THE
SAUSAGE-MAKING
COOKBOOK

The Sausage-Making Cookbook

Jerry Predika

Stackpole Books

Published by
STACKPOLE BOOKS
5067 Ritter Road
Mechanicsburg, PA 17055

Printed in the U.S.A.

Library of Congress Cataloging in Publication Data
Predika, Jerry.
    The sausage-making cookbook.
    1. Sausages. 2. Cookery (Sausages) I. Title.
TX749.P725 1983   641.6'6   82-19679
ISBN 0-8117-1693-7

"THANKS GRAM"

Contents

There was a young lady of Twickenham,
Who of sausage never grew sick of 'em,
She knelt down on the sod
And prayed to her God,
To lengthen, strengthen, and Thickenham.

English Limerick

Introduction

I WAS BORN into a family of Russian and Slavic descendants all of whom, including my parents, came to America from the Old Country. They brought with them many cultural traditions that still remain steadfast within our family. When an occasion to celebrate comes along, it inevitably brings with it much hustle and bustle in the kitchen in preparation for the event.

As far back as I can remember, celebrating Russian Christmas and Russian Easter at my grandparents' house were times I looked forward to with great excitement. The fantastic array of food prepared for the "big day" has always been a centerpoint of attraction. The table groans mightily with many traditional dishes, the most popular being my grandmother's homemade sausage. It invariably took preference on everyone's plate!

The years moved on and her delectable sausage never faultered in remaining number one in the taste treat department. As Gram grew older, and my observations keener, I found to my amazement that she was the only one who knew the recipes. Quite frankly, I became panic-stricken when I realized how many beautiful gourmet treats are lost at death. Sort of like . . . "Gee, I haven't had anything that compares with Aunt Martha's home-made pickled herring since she passed on. Remember how great she used to make it!"

I found myself helping Gram in the kitchen during these special days of celebration and gradually learned some wonderful old-world recipes from her. She made her sausage with such love, and she was a delight to behold, all rosy-cheeked and smiling. As I watched her, I would write down her methods of preparation which she, in fact, had learned from her own mother years before in Russia.

Sausage held a very special interest for me. As it turned out, the more I inquired about the making of sausage and salami other than my Gram's way, the more I found the recipes to be highly guarded or forgotten. Most of the people that I got any information from had come over from Europe, as had my own family, but had given in to the American way of doing things. Time fades memories, and most of the recipes I tracked down were generally rather sketchy.

The big manufacturers have pretty much taken over sausage production in this country and keep their secrets very well indeed. You may be lucky enough to find a sausage shopkeeper who still makes his own sausage, no doubt of a simple variety. In my own endeavors to find enlightenment on sausage making for my own use, I cursed many times over that a book had not been written on the subject. "What a beautiful art," I thought to myself, "and it's dying out!"

I suddenly felt a great challenge and set out determined to write about the subject so that others like myself would have a reference source available to them. I sincerely hope that you will be able to find what you are searching for in its contents.

1

The History of Sausage

THE HISTORY OF sausage making is a most interesting one. The word sausage is derived from the Latin word *salsus*, literally meaning salted or preserved. Sausages and salamis were originally made out of bare necessity, like clothes and shelter, as a way of preserving meat without refrigeration. The earliest reference I could find was from the Greek poet, Homer, who wrote about 2,800 years ago of roasting sausage in the *Odyssey*. Homer describes the wanderings of Odysseus and his decision to cook up a batch of sausage.

Sausage was made and devoured in huge amounts by the Babylonians some 1,500 years ago. The Greeks had a name for it—*oryae*—and had specific names for other types of preserved meats also. Fifth century B.C. literature refers to salami, a sausage which is thought to have originated in the city of Salamis on the east coast of Cyprus.

1

As sausage became popular, Epicharmus wrote a play called *Orya*, which in plain English means *The Sausage*. Around 228 A.D. someone got the brilliant idea of writing a cookbook, and what did it have in it?—sausage recipes! The odd thing is that in present times, there are few cookbooks around that have sausage-making recipes in them. Recipes using sausage, yes! How to make it yourself, no!

The discovery of various spices which helped to preserve meat and enhance flavor prompted the development of a tasty, appetizing food now popularly known as dry sausage. Spices were widely used in the preparation of many foods, and the demand for them grew steadily. Huge trade empires resulted from this cry for spices and other popular goods which in turn led to wars, piracy, and four centuries of struggle. Christopher Columbus went in search of new trade routes to the Orient. Marco Polo, Vasco DaGama, Magellan, and Hendrick Hudson explored the waters to discover the shortest route to the East. Practically every country in the world has its own type of sausage, whether the recipes were stolen from their neighbors and changed, or they were totally concocted on their own.

The sausage makers of small farm villages were developing their own distinctive type of sausage. Of course, there were various contributing factors that made each village's sausage unique in its own taste. Custom, availability of ingredients, and climate were great influences.

Just for instance, Northern Europe had periods of cold weather during which fresh or semifresh meat products would keep. The process of smoking meat developed in this area as a means of aiding in the preservation of meat. In comparison, Southern Europe is hot, you bet! Consequently, this particular part of Europe developed the dry sausage which did not need any refrigeration at all. The Italian climate encouraged the growth of many, and I mean many, different dry sausages. What the whole thing boils down to is the fact that people living in particular areas grew fond of certain types of sausage, and the method of preparation became standardized within that town or community. You can readily see how each place developed its own traditions.

And that brings us to a little tidbit of information which you may already know. The popular sausages of this day and age derive their names from those villages I previously mentioned or, in some cases, huge cities. Bologna originated in the town of Bologna in Northern Italy; Thuringia sausage from the German province of Thuringia; Berliner from its home city of Berlin in Germany; Genoa salami from Genoa; Lyons sausage from Lyons, France; Milano sausage came from Milan, Italy and so on.

The American Indian aided in the widespread popularity of sausage also. He mixed chopped dried buffalo or venison meat with dried berries and shaped the mixture into cakes for use later on in the year. The American pioneers did their part too, bringing their own recipes with them from across the Atlantic. Not having a large variety of spices available .to them before coming to America, they created new sausages upon arrival.

The Immigrant movement of the 1900s brought many new taste changes to this country. Numerous small sausage shops opened to cater to the quickening of tastebuds and, before any time at all, many of the small shops had expanded into what are now known as large national sausage corporations. And do you know what? Their sausages are generally pretty good, though they don't begin to compare in any way, shape, or form to the good old homemade variety.

I suppose I could go on and on, as the background of sausage making is indeed fascinating. However, for my purposes, I think what I have passed on to you thus far has gotten the point across. Sausage has been around for a long time!

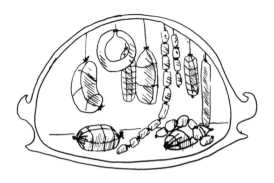

2

Kinds of Sausage

I THINK IF you can understand the classification of the types of sausage, this will aid you in preparing and preserving your own sausage. You will also gain a clearer understanding of commercial labeling.

Fresh Sausage

Made from meats, mainly pork and beef, that have not been previously cured, being neither cooked nor smoked. It should be refrigerated and always thoroughly cooked before serving. Includes fresh pork sausage, Italian pork sausage, fresh country-style pork sausage, fresh beef sausage.

Fresh Smoked Sausage

Just what the name implies . . . fresh sausage that has been smoked, although not cooked like fresh sausage. It should be refrigerated and thoroughly cooked before serving. Varieties include Mettwurst, country-style pork sausage, Roumanian sausage.

Cooked Sausage

Prepared with fresh meats, then thoroughly cooked and ready to serve to anxiously awaiting mouths! This type of sausage must also be refrigerated. Includes veal sausage, liver sausage, Braunschweiger.

Cooked Smoked Sausage

Prepared from fresh meat and both cooked and smoked. They are then ready to eat, either hot or cold. Heating before serving definitely enhances the flavor, but they are good served cold also. Kinds include weiners, bologna (try heating it, you'll like it!), Kielbaza, Vienna sausage.

Dry and Semidry Sausage

Made from selected meats and prepared in a more complicated manner than other types of sausage. The drying process must be very carefully controlled. These sausages are ready to eat and will keep just about forever if refrigerated. Varieties are Italian salami, German salami, summer sausage.

3

Grinders

IN THE EARLY days of my sausage-making career, I learned to make sausage without a grinder. My grandmother and I would sit in the basement cutting the pork into small cubes. In fact, most of the neighbors did it the same way.

It wasn't until I decided to make a variety of sausages that a grinder became a necessity. Not 100% however. I know your friendly butcher will grind the meat for you. There's a good chance you'll be charged for the service, maybe not. It depends on whether it's a Mom and Pop store and how often you shop there. Or you can have the meat ground at one of those large, impersonal supermarket chains . . . check it out if you have no grinder or have no interest in getting one, or you just have too much meat to grind. I've done it!

For serious sausage makers, one of the few items that you will definitely have to acquire in your sausage-making ventures is a

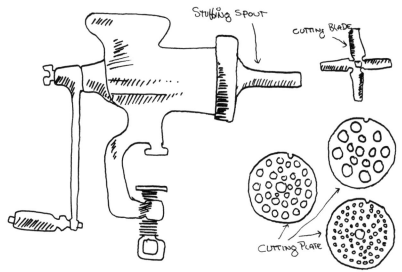

Grinder, Cutting Blade, Cutting Plates and Stuffing Attachments (these are your basic needs)

grinder. When purchasing a grinder, get one that is a bit bigger than your needs to give you room for expansion. Shop around until you find it . . . there are some good deals at yard sales and flea markets. What are you looking for? You're looking for a meat grinder that has at least four cutting plates which come with the grinder or can be purchased later. The four plates range in size from three-fourths of an inch (coarse), three-eighths of an inch (medium-coarse), three-sixteenths (medium) and one-eighth inch (fine). Make sure it comes with a sausage-stuffing attachment and that you can get different sized stuffing attachments. Lamb casing is much smaller than hog casing, therefore it's impossible to put lamb casing on a spout designed for hog casing. Make sure you can get spouts for hog and lamb casing.

You will find all kinds of grinders available once you begin your search. Do consider your own personal needs and, of course, your pocketbook. Sears & Roebuck offers a manual grinder that costs about $25.00 and J. C. Penney offers a similar model. Both

Electric Meat Chopper (not really necessary unless you plan on making many pounds of sausage at one time).

come with five cutting plates and a stuffing attachment. The Sears grinder does a fine job; I have one myself and it handles just about anything I throw into it, including my hand! If you think your arm will fall off from the strain of working the manual grinder and if you plan to make a lot of sausage at one time, invest in a good electric model. Don't settle for a cheap one . . . you'll be sorry. Beware of those toy suction cups grinders that fall apart or the motor burns out before your first sausage is completed. I now own a Holbert Kitchen Aid Mixer-Grinder. That hand grinder was getting too small . . . I had put a lot of meat through it.

The hand grinder is an all-in-one machine. It grinds and stuffs the casing. I've used it this way for years and have always been totally delighted with the end results. Don't forget when you're using a meat grinder to stuff the casing, remove the cutting plate and blade before you start stuffing. If you get into making large volumes of sausage, this kind of grinder tends to slow you down.

Did you know there are other ways of filling the casing once the meat has been chopped or ground? Some are the primitive methods; if you please. Using that strange funnel in the middle of an Angel Food cake pan, or a kitchen funnel, push the meat

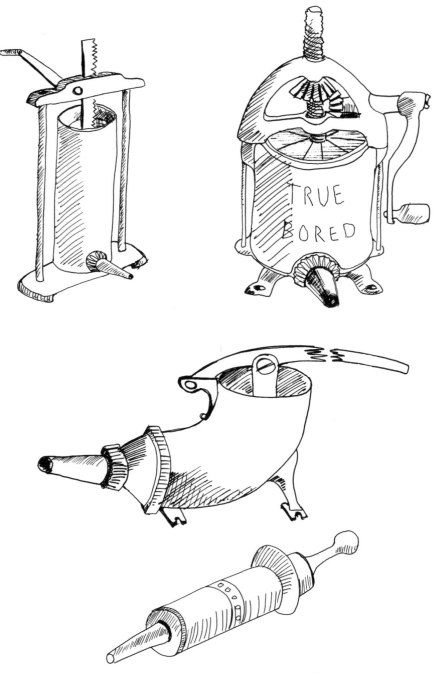

They may look strange, but they're fast and efficient.

through with a wooden spoon. It works all right, with a certain amount of effort.

Strangely enough, the machines for stuffing sausage have not improved much over the last hundred years or so. I guess the marketplace for home sausage makers is a pretty small one. Ah, but it's improving!

I used my Sears grinder to stuff sausage for years . . . and then I ran across a sausage stuffer, also known as a lard or fruit press, at a very good price. There is also a machine known as the sausage funnel, whose entire function is to fill those little casings with a taste delight. Both these machines push or inject the meat into the casing under pressure. Both work very well and I would never go back to the old method.

A new Old Sausage Lard Press is about $250.00. If you can find a used one at a junk store you might be able to get it for $45.00 to $60.00. Cumberland General Store (Route 3, Crossville, Tennessee 38555) stocks them and you can buy parts there as well. They also have a good selection of meat grinders and sausage funnels ranging from $45.00 to $100.00.

In addition to the grinders and stuffers already mentioned, there are two meat choppers I'd recommend: The Chop-rite and The Universal. It's possible to order different sized cutting plates, as well as a variety of sausage cones and replacement parts that somehow always get broken. Prices range from $27.00 to $100.00.

You can find grinders at most department stores, hardware stores, restaurant supply houses, and, of course, garage/yard sales.

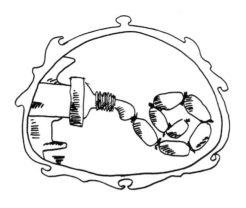

4

Casings

WHEN THIS INGENIOUS food called sausage made its debut a few hundred years ago, I hear tell the first casings were made from the skins of chicken necks. Later on, as man became more imaginative, he used the gut, bowels, or intestines of sheep, hogs and cattle, whichever you prefer, into which he stuffed this wonderful concoction of muscle, herbs, and spices. Yes, I know what you're thinking, believe me, the sausage casings are thoroughly cleaned and packed in salt or salt brine, which keeps them fresh for a very long time.

Casings come in a variety of sizes and are sold by the hank or bundle or the ounce. A hank or bundle is approximately 100 yards and can stuff approximately 100 to 125 pounds of meat if you are using medium-size hog casing, or 40 to 50 pounds if you are using medium-size lamb casing. There is really no way to determine how much casing you will need unless you know the diameter; however, I will give an educated guess—one pound of sausage meat will stuff approximately 1½ to 2 feet of medium-size hog casing (32–35 mm); double that number for medium-size lamb casing (20–22 mm). One ounce of medium hog casing will stuff approximately eight feet of sausage meat; double that for lamb casing.

There are specific types of sausage that use specific types of casing, but you will find that medium size hog or lamb should cover almost all your needs.

Types of Casing

Beef Bungs, Rounds, and Casing

Are used for sausages that require thicker casing than usual such as bologna, liverwurst, Braunschweiger, Mettwurst, cooked salami, and others.

Lamb and Sheep Casing

Are used mostly for country farmstyle sausage or breakfast sausage, also frankfurters and fresh pork sausage. Lamb and sheep casing are very tender. Sheep stomach is used when making a Scottish blood pudding called Haggis and also in a few other recipes in this book.

Hog Casing

Is the most widely used casing in sausage making, and you will no doubt find this type the easiest to find for your own use. Hog casing can be used for just about any sausage, and it is.

Muslin Casing

Is called for in some sausage recipes; mainly in the production of Braunschweiger, liverwurst, blood sausage, salamis, and bo-

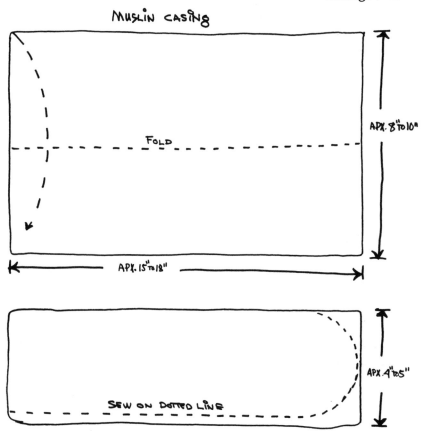

MUSLIN CASING

FOLD

APX. 8" to 10"

APX. 15" to 18"

APX. 4" to 5"

SEW ON DOTTED LINE

lognas. It is made out of strong muslin which seals in the rich flavor of the meat. This type of casing can be easily made at home by stitching strips of muslin to form bags about 2" wide by 15" long. The bags should be dipped in water and wrung out before they are used and must be stuffed when still moist.

Cellulosic Casing

Is artificially made and very difficult to find. It is made from a special grade of cotton linters which are solubilized and regenerated into casing. This type of casing does have the advantages of being uniform, flexible, less breakable, and generally freer of bacterial contamination than other types of casing. Skinless hot dogs are presently made with this kind of casing by the large manufacturers.

Collagen Casing

Is the gelatinous substance found in the connective tissue, bones, and cartilage of all mammals. This is extracted, broken down into simple components, and put back together in the form of casing. This casing is for commercial manufacturers; it's just not available in small quantities. Incidentally, 75% of all sausage made in the United States is stuffed in collagen casing.

Fibrous Casing

Are used for dry and semidry sausage. They have tiny fibers running the length of the casing for added strength. You can stuff salami and other sausage meats much tighter in this type of casing without breaking it; also the inside surface is coated with protein so it will shrink with the meat as it dries out.

Synthetic Casing

Was invented a few years back for use in making pork sausage. It is used mainly by the producers of sausage and is made from alginates. Yes, you've seen it. It's the red casing used for bologna, white for liverwurst, and clear for cooked salami. This casing requires no refrigeration; I guess you might say it's plastic, ah but it's not!

Anyway, these synthetic casings have proven themselves for the commercial manufacturers. They have wonderful machinability and they are uniform in size to insure exact portion control. Using synthetic casings saves time and gives the manufacturer a greater profit margin, allowing him to make more sausage.

Obtaining the Casing

It is unlikely that you will be able to find casing in a conventional store. You may have to look for awhile, as it is sometimes difficult to find. I suggest that you try stores patronized by foreign-born shoppers or a market that features its own sausage. There is also the chance that your local butcher can order it. In any case, don't give up! This is obviously a necessary item for sausage making.

Once you have found a source for casing, you will notice it will be either covered with salt or soaking in brine. Before using the casing, soak it in warm water for 30 or 40 minutes and flush it out immediately before stuffing. That is, put one end over the tip of the water faucet and let the water run through. Storing the casing overnight seems to make it more tender. It is also a good idea to pour a cup of vinegar through the casing so that the sausage will keep better, although this is not absolutely necessary. In the event you have any casing left over, rinse it off, pack it in salt and refrigerate. It will keep for months.

Making Your Own Casing

For you pioneer-spirited people who happen to be butchering your own hogs and would like to use the intestines for casings, be sure the bowel parts are still warm when you begin this procedure. Cut the intestines off at the stomach, pull them out until you reach the large intestine, then cut this part off. You will be using only the small intestine. Remove all ruffle fat (this pulls right off). Wash and clean the intestine carefully. Reverse by turning up a fold at the end of the intestine as you would in making a cuff on a pair of pants. Pour warm water into the cuff. The weight of the water will pull the intestine through.

At this point in the procedure you will need some extra manpower. Get one person to hold the gut, one to pour the water, and one to feed the gut through. Feel free to cut the intestine at lengths that will be easiest for you to handle while making your casing. The mucous membranes are now on the outside and should be scraped off well with the back of a knife. Repeat the scraping procedure several times in order to insure thorough cleansing. Re-turn the casing after washing in warm water, then wash again. Pack it in dry salt, put it in a plastic bag, and store it in the refrigerator until you are ready to use it. Just like that!

5

Preparing the Meat

The Cuts of Meat

The cuts of meat I've used in the recipes in this book I feel are the best and most economical cuts available today for making sausage.

Pork

Boston butt or shoulder comes with a bone or without, it's a little more costly without the bone of course. This cut seems to have a good balance of fat-to-lean ratio. You may run across a recipe that calls for 3 pounds of lean pork and 1 pound of pork fat. I've made it easy; they're talking about Boston butt or shoulder. It's just alot easier to buy Boston butt than to look for lean pork and pork fat. Sausage making should be fun, not frustrating. However, if you really want to look for pig snout, ears, belly fat, and fat back, write me a letter. I'll gladly send you some recipes.

Beef

Chuck roast, 7-bone roast, blade cut roast, pot roast or anything from the chuck or shoulder of beef works just fine. Again, it has the proper amount of fat.

Veal

Any cut of veal that you can afford will do just fine. Sausage needs fat; I would guess somewhere in the area of 25% to 30% fat in one form or another. Don't make it lean or you will be disappointed with the results.

Grinding the Meat

Those are the three basic meats used for making fresh sausage. These meats must be kept as cold as possible during the sausage-making process. The meat should be cut to fit the grinder and stored in the freezer or refrigerator after each step. It is important to have the meat as stiff as possible without freezing it, before putting it in the grinder. The reason for this is that soft meat can be crushed and the juices will run out. Firm meat is cut and retains the juices and solidness of the meat. Also, I might add, since the meat has been ground, there is more surface area for bacteria to start. Again, keep it very cold.

After grinding the meat, put it in the freezer or refrigerator. Then clean up the mess and get ready for the next step.

You will notice that all the recipes call for some liquid to be added. I suggest adding one or two beef or vegetable bouillon cubes to one cup water. However, that's up to you. It does make a difference.

Spices

Using the freshest spices possible, combine them in a bowl or plastic bag, making sure they are thoroughly mixed. There are three ways of handling the spicing of the sausage

1) Adding to the cubed meat before it's ground, then grinding with the spice
2) Adding the premixed spice to the already ground meat
3) Mixing the premixed spice into the water used in the recipe—letting it stand about an hour and adding it to the ground meat

The idea is to get the spices thoroughly mixed into the ground meat. The water helps in that process. Make sure all the spices are mixed throughout the meat, then put the meat back in the freezer or refrigerator and warm up your hands. Mixing sausage meat is not a spoon job, it's a hand job, and it's cold, and it better be.

PLEASE KEEP IN MIND, IF YOU ARE MAKING FRESH PORK SAUSAGE, *DO NOT TASTE.* SMELLING IT IS FINE, TRICHINOSIS IS NOT SO FINE.

Stuffing the Casing

Remove enough casing from the salt or brine for your needs and soak it in water. Don't worry if you soak too much casing. You can simply drain off what you don't use, cover it with salt and refrigerate. I keep my casing in a plastic bag in the refrigerator and have never had a problem.

Rinse out the casing, open the end, and slip it over the sausage horn. Push the casing toward the stuffing machine. Remember to keep some water in the casing, it works as a lubricant when you put the sausage on the horn and when you take it off. It should be pushed back until it forms an accordion-like pleat. Leave about three inches of casing hanging over the horn. Force some sausage meat through the casing, then push the meat back

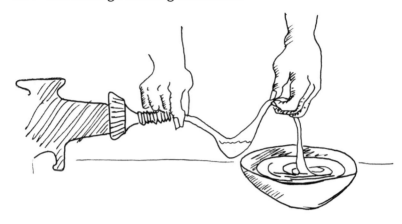

Make sure there is some water in the casing as you put it onto the spout.

into the horn with your fingers, and tie a knot. This is to remove the air from the stuffing horn. Once this is done, you're on your way . . . well, almost!

While the casing is being filled with the sausage mixture, you will find that it will ease off the spout without too much effort on your part. As a matter of fact, it may come off too easily. You'll just have to learn with experience how to regulate the flow of the casing to insure a tightly packed sausage. Hold the casing on the stuffing horn with your thumb and forefinger. This enables you to regulate the flow of casing by increasing or decreasing pressure on the casing. It won't take long before you will develop the expertise to insure a tightly packed sausage.

In the event the casing bursts, stop and tie off the sausage at the breaking point, and continue to stuff the unused portion of the casing.

As the sausage is formed, you may tie the ends or make links. Links are formed by twisting the sausage at various intervals as it comes off the stuffing horn. The size of the links will generally be determined by the type of sausage that you are making, although you should feel free to vary the size of the links to

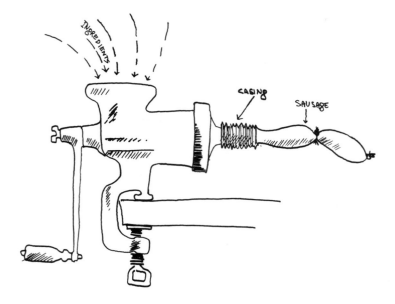

Grinder with casing attached, in the process of being stuffed

your own likes. If a more uniform link is desired, mark on a cutting board the length you want, stuff the sausage loosely, and make one long sausage. Lay the sausage out on the cutting board and use the marks on the board for a guide. Make sure to squeeze the sausage a little at each link and twist. Cotton string can also be used to make links. I don't particularly care for string on fresh sausage.

Storing the Sausage

After stuffing the sausage into the casing, place it overnight in the refrigerator or hang in a cooler to insure proper blending of the spices. Fresh sausage or fresh-smoked sausage will keep approximately one week if refrigerated. If frozen, you can figure it will keep for at least two to four months.

The best way I've found to freeze sausage and retain its original flavor for a long period of time is to put it in a freezer bag, immerse the bag in water until all or most of the air is pushed out, then twist and tie the bag. Put another bag over the first and repeat. You see, the air is the problem and will suck the flavors from your freshly made sausage. As far as that goes, frozen air will suck the flavor from anything.

When you place the sausage in the freezer, make sure each package is separate from the other. The sausage should freeze as fast and as uniformly as possible. Stacking the packages on top of each other hinders the freezing process.

Also, when you're ready to thaw the meat, do it slowly and don't leave it in the sun or dump it in hot water. Remove the package from the freezer and refrigerate it for approximately 24 hours. It thaws slowly and tastes great!!!

One of the oldest methods of keeping sausage fresh, which is still being used today, is the lard-and-crock method. To do this, partially fry the sausage, place it in a stone crock, and cover it completely with melted lard. It will keep fresh for a very long time this way. The real fun comes when you try to dig the sausage out! I personally do not recommend this method.

6

What You Can Do Without

Spoilage

I am sure everyone has experienced some food spoilage of one type or another whether it was curdled milk, green cheese, or sticky hamburger. It's all the same . . . it's spoiled.

Spoiled food is caused by minute living bodies, not perceptible to the naked eye. They are known as microorganisms and include bacteria, protozoans, viruses, mold and yeast, to name a few.

Mold

A downy or furry growth on the surface of organic matter. You know, it's that green stuff you've seen growing on old cheese and bread.

Yeast

A unicellular fungus which reproduces by budding; that's why it's put into bread dough. Yeast is also capable of fermenting carbohydrates (sugar).

Bacteria

There are three main forms of bacteria: sperical (cocci), rod-shaped (bacilli) and spiral (spirilla). These are the critters that will give you the most trouble in the kitchen and yes, they are everywhere. Staphylococcal food poisoning, salmonellosis and clostridium botulinum are the worst of all food poisons. They can all cause serious illness, as well as death.

Staphylococcal Food Poisoning

A toxin produced by the staphylococci. When ingested, it causes nausea, vomiting, intestinal cramps . . . the works. Attacks usually last three to six hours, fatalities are rare . . . who needs it!

Salmonellosis

An infection by a rod-shaped bacteria, salmonella, which causes intestinal inflammation and diseases of the genital tract.

Clostridium Botulinum

A poisoning resulting from the toxin produced by a certain bacillus. Sometimes found in foods improperly preserved. Often results in death . . . I know I don't need that!

Microorganisms are carried by many sources. There's your pet dog or cat. And then there's the person who coughs into his hand and then shakes hands with your favorite chef, who in turn prepares your lunch. Ah! and let's not forget the infamous housefly who picks up microorganisms, flies into you-know-who's house, and lands on you-know-what. Bacteria gets passed around and there's no way to avoid it.

It is impossible to rid the atmosphere completely of these organisms, but we can keep them down to a minimum. Make sure everything is clean, including your hands and your clothes. Keep your work area uncluttered and don't let things stand around that the flies might like.

Don't make sausage in the heat of the day. The meat has to be kept ice cold. Work fast! If the meat warms up, you're asking for trouble. Put that sausage in the refrigerator as soon as it's done. Don't let it stack up. Clean up as you go . . .

You should be getting my point:

> get it done,
>> cold,
>> clean,
>> and
>> fast.

Trichinosis

Trichinosis, that's a word I've heard ever since I was a kid in Ohio, and I think everyone in my neighborhood did. I'm not sure if I ever understood what it was, but it sure scared the pants off me!

I knew it was one of those things that if you didn't cook the pork thoroughly, you would be eaten alive from the inside out by all kinds of hungry worms—it still gives me the shivers when I think about it.

Since then, I've found out a bit more information on the subject.

Trichinosis is a disease that comes from eating infected and undercooked pork and bear meat. It is caused by a tiny round worm, the *Trichinella spiralis* or, trichina which enters an animal's system through its food. Pigs are most commonly infected with this parasite if they are fed uncooked garbage containing scraps of uncooked pork from, of course, other infected pigs—it's a vicious circle. The trichina attaches itself to the walls of the intestines. Its offspring then bore into the walls of the intestine, then enter the blood vessels and are carried to the muscles where they roll up and form hard capsules or cysts. After a year or so the cysts harden and the worms die.

As long as you have not ingested more infected pork, you may rid yourself of this problem. The majority of patients do recover. However, when large numbers of trichina have been ingested and find their way to the respiratory muscles, the infection then becomes very serious and fatal.

Symptoms of trichinosis in the first few days are headaches, fever, serious diarrhea, nausea, swollen and painful eyes, and vomiting. In about one week, muscular symptoms develop; muscles become swollen, firm, and extremely painful.

The treatment for trichinosis is, in a general symptomatic and supportive way, to enable the patient to survive the acute pain and poisoning following the invasion of the muscles. There is no treatment for trichinosis . . .

To avoid trichinosis, follow these simple rules. The parasite is destroyed at a temperature of 138° F. So when you fry, bake, barbecue, broil, or boil the pork sausage, it should reach an internal temperature of 138° F. In using pork meat in dried sausages such as hard salami or pepperoni, this is the rule—drying the meat does not kill the trichina worm. You must freeze the pork and maintain a certain temperature. Make sure the meat is no thicker than five inches. I suggest cubing it in one inch cubes. Follow these specifications: at −5° F. you must freeze for 20 days, at −10° F. it's 10 days, and −20° F., 6 days. This should take care of any potential problems.

You can also buy prefrozen pork known as Certified Pork, which has undergone the freezing treatment to eliminate the parasite. Ask your butcher to order it and he may give you a strange look. Ask around, it's a little frustrating I know, but when you do find it, make sure it's stamped or labeled "Certified Pork."

Additives

Nitrates and Nitrites

Both nitrates and nitrites are used in the production and preservation of cured meat products such as ham, bacon, and frankfurters. They are vital ingredients in cured meat because they prevent the growth of the toxin-producing strain of clostridium botulinum sometimes present in raw or cooked meat, and they add months to the shelf life of cured meat products.

We always thought that nitrates were only in bacon, frankfurters, or some kind of processed meat. Boy, do I have news for you. Man is exposed to nitrates and nitrites everyday even without eating one single hotdog. Nitrates are present naturally in the soil, the water, all plant materials, the atmosphere, and in meat. However, the concentration is usually very low, with the exception of well water.

In healthy individuals, nitrates and nitrites are rapidly absorbed from the gastrointestinal tract into the blood. Absorbed nitrite reacts with the hemoglobin to form methemoglobin which, in adults, is rapidly converted to oxyhemoglobin and excreted by the kidneys.

However, in some infants up to six months old the enzyme system is not completely developed and the methemoglobin is unable to be converted to oxyhemoglobin. The result is methemoglobinemia, a condition which occurs where the hemoglobin fails to transport oxygen throughout the body, and sometimes leads to death.

The possible health hazards from nitrites and nitrates are up for question. It is a fact that methemoglobinemia is a byproduct of nitrates and nitrites and can cause death and has done so in the past, no matter what the age of the victim. Are nitrites and nitrates carcinogenic? Who knows, the mice aren't talking about it. Although there is no clinical evidence, I wouldn't be surprised.

Nitrates and nitrites seem to be everywhere, whether I like it or not. I do have control over my own sausage and I elect not to add them. However, if you feel compelled, add at the rate of

6.1 grams per 100 pounds of meat, just short of a teaspoon. It doesn't seem like much, but it's too much for me.

There are commercial cures in the marketplace, and they all contain nitrates and nitrites. Follow the instructions closely . . . if you have good reason to use them. My advice is to leave them out.

Saltpeter

Oh, the tales that go along with saltpeter.

Saltpeter, the common name for potassium nitrate, has no value whatsoever as a preservative nor any nutritional value. Its value is purely aesthetic. What saltpeter really does is keep the meat nice and rosy red, and nothing else.

Add about one-half teaspoon per five pounds of meat. Adding more will only toughen the meat. Adding sugar will correct some of that problem but you can add only so much sugar (about one-half teaspoon per pound).

If you want rosy red sausage, add some sweet paprika or crystalline ascorbic acid, which is a form of Vitamin C (about one-fourth teaspoon per five pounds of meat). It will keep it pink, although the color won't last forever. You can get it at most drugstores.

There is also another kind of saltpeter available. This is chilean saltpeter, chemically known as sodium nitrate. It's not the same as potassium nitrate and serves no purpose in sausage making. Don't be confused.

7

Smoked Sausage

THE SMOKING OF meat seems to have started quite accidentally. Neolithic man built smudge fires under their drying racks to keep the flies away from the meat as it dried in the sun. Through the use of fire, they soon realized that the meat was drying faster, keeping for longer periods of time, and the flavor was much improved.

Later on, the application of salt to the meat was introduced and the brine cure came close behind. These new methods added even more to the flavor and preserving qualities of the meat.

Smoking and salting meat became an important and widely-used preserving process. Meat and fish were heavily salted and then smoked for many weeks. These were the days before refrigeration and transportation was slow. Armies on long campaigns and seamen aboard ships for many months preserved their meat and fish in this manner.

Today meat is smoked and salt-cured to add *flavor*, and not to preserve the meat. Large manufacturers of sausage rely on chemical preservatives of one kind or another. These chemicals I can do without, and I'm sure many of you will agree! I prefer the old traditional method; preserving *can* still be done naturally.

What Is Smoke?

It is strange to think of smoke as a preservative, but hiding in the clouds of smoke are tiny droplets of various natural chemicals such as aldehydes, phenols, ketones, and carbolic acid. These chemicals condense on the food being smoked. Some will be absorbed into the liquid of the meat and will make their way into the meat itself. Others will settle on the meat surface, giving a wonderful smoky flavor. These natural chemicals also kill or check the formation of bacteria, yeast, and mold microorganisms which are the little devils that start decay. Phenols in the smoke prevent the oils and fats from turning rancid. Do keep in mind that smoking will *not* turn deteriorating meat into some mouth-watering tidbit. If you begin with bad meat, you will invariably end up with bad meat!

Smoking Sausage

Most fresh and dried sausage is smoked to add flavor, not to dry the meat. When making smoked fresh sausage, add a little more salt to the mixture and refrigerate for 24 hours, with the seasonings being added before stuffing into the casing. The sausage should hang-dry before smoking to prevent a mottled surface. Smoke to a dark mahogany color or to your own taste. Be sure to refrigerate this type of sausage shortly after you remove it from the smokehouse.

If you're making dry sausage, the drying is accomplished by cool air, so smoke it sufficiently for flavor and then hang in a cool place to dry slowly. If you want to dry your sausage in the smokehouse with smoke, fine! Dry with a temperature not exceeding 90° F. until the sausage is adequately dried. Providing the meat has been properly cured, it will be ready to eat when completely dry and will keep without refrigeration. Dry sausage may be heated before eating if desired.

The amount of time you smoke your sausage will depend entirely upon your own tastes. If smoking in a hog casing, about 15 hours at 90° F. should do the job. If the meat is encased in muslin bags, you may take it out of the smokehouse when the bags have turned a rich dark brown color. That should do it for the average taste.

Experiment with the amount of time you smoke your sausage, then you'll know what's just right for you. Cut a piece of the meat off, cook it, try it! If you find it not to be smoked enough, put it back into the smokehouse and smoke the meat for a few hours, or however long you wish. Keep in mind too much smoke can be unpalatable. Try to keep the smoke going continuously. The smoke is what keeps the bacteria out of the meat. Sausage hanging around at 90° F. are perfect places for bacteria to grow. Smoke it as soon as possible. Ah, don't rush though! If you raise the temperature too fast, the sausage will perspire, causing uneven smoking and mottling. And don't start with a high temperature when you're hot smoking, do it in steps starting around 120° F. The casing has to be firmly dry; if not, the grease will ooze from the sausage, giving it a lard stick look. Make sure the sausage don't touch one another.

Try to keep a record of the type of meat, weight, smoking time, type of wood, and the seasonings used. You will find your notes to be invaluable in the long run. When smoking sausage, all the preserving salt and spices have already been added to the meat. Making dry and semidry sausage involves a special dry-curing process that will cure the meat during its drying period.

There are two basic methods of smoking: hot-smoking and cold-smoking, which is just plain old smoking. Hot-smoked sausage is both flavored and cooked with hot smoke. After removing from the smokehouse, shower them with cold water. Why?—It keeps the meat from shriveling up. If the sausage should become shriveled, cook them in hot water to bring back the firmness and then shower in cold water.

Since hot-smoked sausage is not entirely dried out, and frequently may be moist and juicy, their keeping qualities are limited. Unless refrigerated or frozen, they should be consumed within a few days after processing. A quicker alternative method to hot-smoking, sometimes used by British sausage-makers, requires cooking the sausage in hot water at about 180° F. for 65 minutes, then smoking until the desired color is attained. What I'm talking about are sausages like frankfurters, bologna, polish sausage, to name a few.

Sausage is cold-smoked for flavor only. You can start with either fresh or dried sausage. Cold-smoking improves flavor and tends to preserve the sausage by inhibiting the bacterial action.

Some Chorizo, Kosher style beef sausage, and fresh pork sausage are a few fresh sausages that are cold-smoked. Sausages like pepperoni, hard salami and Genoa salami are some of the dried cured sausages.

Building Your Own Smokehouse

Your smokehouse can be constructed of just about anything that will hold smoke: wood barrels, steel drums, old iceboxes or refrigerators, cardboard boxes, bricks, plywood, or whatever else you can think up! Guess you could say anything that will hold smoke, period. The smoke can come from a fire placed a good ten or twelve feet away from the smokehouse itself or from a hot plate with a pie pan to hold the wood.

There are also a lot of electric home smokers available to the home sausage maker. Most will eliminate the guesswork of smoking sausage, as well as being practical and economical. Actually, they work very well for the small sausage maker.

Here are a few guidelines for building a simple smokehouse, should you decide to build one yourself.

1) It should be of a tight enough construction to hold the smoke and heat.

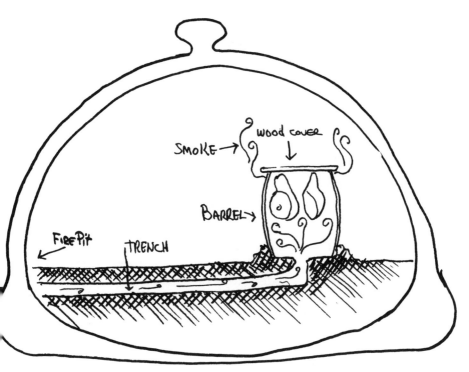

2) A ventilation system to maintain a given temperature like a top and bottom draft should be installed.
3) It should have a heating and smoking system that can be controlled.
4) It should be large enough to hang sausage so they don't touch each other.
5) There should be a way to measure inside temperature.
6) If you decide on a large smokehouse, it should be in a location far enough from your neighbors and yourself.

Here are some details on the construction of a simple barrel smokehouse. This information will give you an idea of how a smokehouse works, thereby giving you a better understanding of how to build one of your own no matter what method you choose.

Find yourself a barrel of about 55 gallon capacity. Knock out both ends of the barrel. If you plan on using this barrel smokehouse as a permanent one, I would suggest drilling holes in the metal bands that hold the thing together. At each wood slat or rib of the barrel put in a wood screw to insure the barrel against

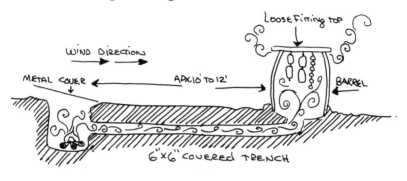

collapsing—that is if you are using a wooden barrel. Dig a hole just a bit narrower than the diameter of the barrel about two feet deep. Nail two wooden strips on both sides of the barrel a few inches from the top to rest the meat racks on. Make a lid or use the one you knocked out, making sure it fits loosely. The smoke, moisture, and heat must escape from the barrel freely.

Dig a trench in the direction of the wind approximately twelve feet from the barrel, connecting one end to the hole and the other to a fire pit which you will dig. Cover the trench to form a chimney, make a lid for the fire pit, and you're on your way!

Keep in mind the location of your smokehouse. Placing it next to the house is not a very good idea. Try to keep it pretty much off by itself. Careful regulations of the air inlets and heat control on the burner will control the temperature and minimize the danger of the wood from flaming up. This could obviously ruin the whole thing, including the meat you're smoking.

A more modern way and a labor-saving method is the double hot plate method, putting the hot plate under the barrel with a No. 10 tin can to hold the wood chips. You must drill approximately eight holes in the bottom of the barrel to allow for the draft. Insert a metal disk just a little smaller than the barrel to fit just the can in case the wood should catch on fire. Regulate the draft by putting corks into the holes you have drilled, and I'm sure you will have success. You may be asking yourself the question, "Why the double hot plate?" This is merely for adding the extra heat for use in kippering or hot-smoking.

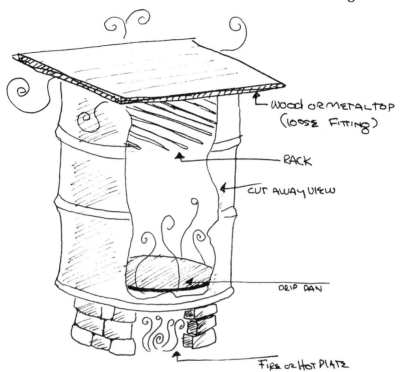

WOOD OR METAL TOP
(LOOSE FITTING)

RACK

CUT AWAY VIEW

DRIP PAN

FIRE OR HOT PLATE

Also, it's not a bad idea to have a three-level heat regulator or thermostat control to adjust the heat. Since the smoker is largely constructed of wood, take precautions not to overheat it. Use a thermometer to maintain the proper temperature. It may be inserted in a cork and put through the side or suspended through a hole in the top of the barrel. Control the ventilation carefully so that the wood smolders and smokes and does *not* produce a flame. If you do happen to use the hot plate method, I suggest that you ground the hot plate to a metal rod driven into the ground or to a water pipe.

Wood to be used in your smokehouse should be nonresinous, such as apple, cherry, alder, oak, maple, ash or hickory! Any resinous wood will blacken the meat and give it an undesirable flavor. Make sure that you remove the bark from the wood before

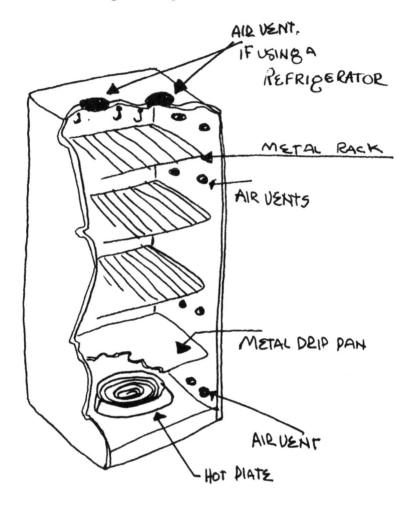

AIR VENT,
IF USING A
REFRIGERATOR

METAL RACK

AIR VENTS

METAL DRIP PAN

AIR VENT

HOT PLATE

you use it. The bark will lend a bitter taste which I am sure you won't like.

Some tips to keep in mind

1) Be sure to preheat your smoker before placing in your meat.

2) Put vegetable oil on the smoking racks and trays so the meat will not stick to them.

3) Make sure the meat is thoroughly dry before putting it into the smokehouse, otherwise it will steam instead of smoke.
4) Fresh meats are always preferable to frozen meats.
5) Watch your fire well; try to avoid open flames.
6) Positively no resinous woods are to be used.

Experiment with your smoker. Taste is an individual matter. Try using small amounts of meat or whatever you happen to be smoking until you become familiar with your smokehouse and your own tastebuds. The whole process of smoking can be lots of fun, lots of work, and worth every minute of the time spent on it! Preseverance is the key, as it is with so many things.

8

About the Recipes

AS YOU EMBARK on your very own sausage-making ventures, you will undoubtedly add your own personal touch to the recipes offered in this book. As with all recipes, eventually one changes them in some way or another to suit one's own individual tastebuds. I hope you will experiment with the following recipes. They are given to you as guides. Many, I feel, will last another thousand years!

Keep things clean. Sterilize the grinder and all utensils that will come in contact with the meat by pouring boiling water over them. Keep your hands clean and washed.

Keep the meat ice cold. Don't let it lay around. This is the perfect place for bacteria to start. Store it in the refrigerator or freezer. Don't freeze it, just keep it stiff. Take special care when using pork, which has a high rate of spoilage.

You will find that your grinder will have a coarse cutting plate and a fine plate, with a few variations in between. When you're making a fine ground sausage, add all the seasonings to the cubed pork and run the meat through the grinder plates two times. Start first with the medium plate, refrigerate the ground meat until it is stiff, then use the fine plate the second time around. Keep that meat ice cold.

In the event you don't have time to grind the meat, or you want to make a large quantity of sausage, ask your butcher to grind it for you. It may cost a little more, who knows. My butcher never charges me for grinding a thing . . . I think it's because I give him a couple of pounds of you-know-what.

Adding soy protein concentrates or nonfat dry milk to your sausage will keep the sausage much more moist and juicy. Add it at a rate of two tablespoons per pound. Generally it's only added to cooked sausage such as frankfurters or bologna. If added to fresh sausage, it will change the appearance a little. It's up to you. Its total function is to retain the moisture from the meat, it's not a filler. You may have to add a little extra water to the recipe.

Don't experiment in cutting back on the fat in order to produce a lean sausage. It will become dry and the texture will be very much like sawdust. If you decide that you do want to cut back on the fat content, do it in moderation and save yourself alot of disappointment.

When putting the spices together, make sure you use the freshest spices you can find. It's a good idea to mix all the spices together and put them into the meat at one time. Please keep in mind that the spices and salt must be thoroughly mixed into the meat mixture. The spices and salt preserve and flavor the meat, which of course is of the utmost importance in producing a good sausage. Without a proper mixing, you will fail in both areas.

As you look over the recipes, you should notice each one has a cup or more of water added to it. Adding two beef bouillon cubes per cup of water will enhance the flavor of the sausage. Yes, I know, grandma didn't do it that way . . . that's why I leave the decision up to you. Incidentally, the reason for the water is that it helps in moving the spices through the meat mixture. Feel free to add more water, but only if it's necessary.

There are products called liquid smoke. This can be added to the sausage meat at a rate of one and one-half teaspoon or more per pound of meat unless the bottle has different instructions.

I tried to standardize these recipes to five pounds. If the recipe is to be increased, don't forget to add just a little bit more seasoning than what was figured. It's the old "one for the pot" philosophy . . . it works!

Pure crystalline ascorbic acid, that's Vitamin C, keeps the sausage looking rosy and pink. If it makes a difference to you, add one fourth teaspoon per five pounds of meat.

Air bubbles are a no-no. The air contains bacteria which can cause spoilage. Removing the air bubbles is simple: take a needle and prick the air pocket. Don't spend an hour with a magnifying glass for the little ones. Prick what you can see and that should do it.

The cutting knife and plates of the grinder must be kept sharp and clean to insure proper cutting of the meat. Don't forget the meat must be firm before putting it into the grinder.

Strangely enough, it's not necessary to have a meat grinder, a sausage press, or hog or lamb casing. What you need is a recipe. Your butcher grinds the meat, you add the seasonings, refrigerate for twenty-four hours, and make into patties or a loaf. I know it's not the same, and certainly has its limitations, but it works!

When the time comes for experimenting, remember . . . approximately one teaspoon of salt per pound of meat, approximately one quarter to one half teaspoon black pepper . . . the rest you can add.

The recipes in this book are a cross section from many parts of the globe: Germany, Russia, Italy, France, America, and so on. They include only a small proportion of sausage recipes still being used throughout the world. They're some of the best.

Cooking Sausage

Thorough cooking is an absolute necessity in preparing fresh pork sausage. Other varieties of sausages do not require cooking, but can be heated if so desired.

It is best to cook the sausage rather gently. Use tongs when turning the links. Try not to pierce the skin. Wonderful juices can be lost if the surface of the sausage is pricked open while cooking.

The following methods of cooking your sausage are recommended.

Pan-fry

Put the sausage in a cold skillet. Add approximately one-half cup of water plus 2 tablespoons vegetable oil or olive oil, and cook slowly over medium-low heat for approximately 10 minutes. The time cooked will depend on the size and thickness of the sausage. Remove cover and brown slowly, cooking until well done.

Pan Broil

Brown sausages in a little fat in a heavy skillet under the broiler unit in your oven. Turn slowly to brown evenly. Cook until done, watching closely to avoid burning.

Bake

Place sausage on a rack in the oven in a shallow baking pan, baking at 375° F. for about 45 minutes, depending on the size of the sausage.

Broil

If desired, brush sausage with butter or margarine. Broil 3 to 4 inches from the broiler unit, turning to check brownness. Broil until done.

Simmer

Place *cooked* sausage links in boiling water, cover and simmer on low heat for 5 to 10 minutes or until thoroughly heated. Don't boil the sausage! A delicious variation is to simmer in wine or beer.

Grill

Brush links with butter, margarine, or olive oil, if desired, and grill over low coals until nicely browned and well done. If grilling fresh link sausages, be sure to boil them first. Place links in water, bring them to a boil, remove from heat, and allow to stand for about 10 minutes before grilling. This is just to make sure they are thoroughly cooked . . . it's not necessary if you can barbecue them slowly.

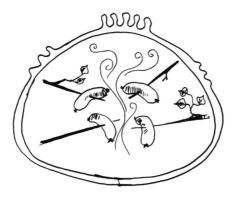

9

Fresh Sausage Recipes

American Beef Sausage

6 lbs. lean ground beef
2 tsp. sage
3 tsp. salt
1½ tsp. freshly ground black
    pepper

1 tsp. cayenne
3 cups bread crumbs
4 Tbsp. parsley, chopped
2 beaten eggs
1 cup water

Mix all ingredients thoroughly and stuff into hog casings. Put into boiling water, being sure to cover completely with water, and boil for about ½ hour. Take from pot and allow to cool, then refrigerate. To serve, cut meat into thin slices and broil slowly until brown on all sides.

AMERICAN

American Country Farm Style Sausage

Add all ingredients, mix well and stuff into small hog or sheep casing, or make into patties. Can also be stuffed into muslin bags.

5 lbs. medium ground pork
   butt
5 tsp. salt
2 Tbsp. sage
1 tsp. ground cloves
3 tsp. black pepper

½ tsp. thyme
½ tsp. allspice
2 finely diced large onions
4 cloves pressed garlic
1 cup cold water

5 lbs. medium ground pork
   butt
5 tsp. salt
2 tsp. black pepper
1 tsp. marjoram

2 tsp. basil
1 tsp. thyme
4 cloves pressed garlic
1 cup cold water

5 lbs. medium ground pork
   butt
1 large diced onion
5 tsp. salt
1½ tsp. black pepper

½ tsp. allspice
½ tsp. cloves
½ tsp. cayenne
1 cup cold water

5 lbs. medium ground pork
   butt
5 tsp. salt
1 Tbsp. black pepper

2 tsp. marjoram
2 tsp. thyme
1½ Tbsp. ground sage
1 cup cold water

5 lbs. medium ground pork
   butt
5 tsp. salt

2½ tsp. ground sage
2½ tsp. black pepper
1 cup cold water

5 lbs. medium ground pork
   butt
5 tsp. salt
1½ tsp. black pepper
1 tsp. cayenne

¾ tsp. allspice
3 tsp. sage
1½ bay leaves
1 cup cold water

3 lbs. *medium ground beef*
   chuck
2 lbs. *medium ground bacon*
5 tsp. *salt*
1 tsp. *pepper*

2 Tbsp. *chopped pimentos*
½ tsp. *savory*
½ tsp. *marjoram*
4 *cloves pressed garlic*
1 *cup cold water*

3 lbs. *medium ground pork*
   butt
2 lbs. *medium ground bacon*
5 tsp. *salt*
2 tsp. *pepper*
1 Tbsp. *chili powder*

1 tsp. *marjoram*
½ tsp. *thyme*
½ tsp. *coriander*
6 *cloves pressed garlic*
1 *cup cold water*

5 lbs. *medium ground pork*
   butt
5 tsp. *salt*
5 tsp. *sage*

1 Tbsp. *black pepper*
2 tsp. *sugar*
1 tsp. *ground nutmeg*
1 *cup cold water*

5 lbs. medium ground pork butt	1 tsp. allspice
5 tsp. salt	½ tsp. ginger
1 Tbsp. sugar	½ tsp. cloves
1 tsp. black pepper	½ tsp. cayenne
	1 cup cold water

5 lbs. medium ground pork butt	½ Tbsp. sage
5 tsp. salt	½ tsp. nutmeg
1 Tbsp. black pepper	1 cup cold water

5 lbs. medium ground pork butt	1 Tbsp. sage
5 tsp. salt	1 Tbsp. marjoram
1½ Tbsp. black pepper	½ grated lemon rind
1½ tsp. thyme	1 cup cold water

5 lbs. medium ground pork
   butt
5 tsp. salt
1 Tbsp. black pepper
1 tsp. cayenne

1 Tbsp. sage
1 tsp. ginger
1 crushed bay leaf
1 cup cold water

5 lbs. medium ground pork
   butt
5 tsp. salt
1 Tbsp. black pepper

1 tsp. ground nutmeg
1 Tbsp. sage
1 tsp. cayenne
1 cup cold water

5 lbs. medium ground pork
   butt
5 tsp. salt
2 tsp. black pepper
1 Tbsp. sage

½ tsp. cloves
1 tsp. mace
½ tsp. nutmeg
1 tsp. grated lemon rind
1 cup cold water

5 lbs. medium ground pork
   butt
5 tsp. salt
1 Tbsp. ground sage

1 Tbsp. black pepper
1 Tbsp. allspice
1 cup cold water

5 lbs. medium ground pork
  butt
5 tsp. salt
1 Tbsp. black pepper

2 Tbsp. sage
1 tsp. cloves
½ tsp. nutmeg
½ tsp. cayenne

5 lbs. medium ground pork
  butt
1⅓ Tbsp. salt
1½ tsp. black pepper
1 tsp. dried thyme

2½ tsp. dried sage
½ tsp. savory
1½ tsp. sugar
1 tsp. crushed red pepper
1 cup cold water

Combine all ingredients, mix well and stuff into sheep casing or make into patties.

3 lbs. medium ground pork
  butt
2 lbs. medium ground veal
3 cups bread crumbs
2 grated lemon rinds
1 tsp. sage
1 tsp. sweet marjoram

1 tsp. thyme
½ tsp. savory
2 tsp. black pepper
1½ Tbsp. salt
½ tsp. nutmeg
1 cup cold water

For a little heat, add 2 tsp. crushed hot peppers. Combine all ingredients, mix well and stuff into sheep casing or make into patties.

5 lbs. medium ground pork butt	2 tsp. sweet marjoram
½ tsp. thyme	1 tsp. crushed bay leaf
1 tsp. savory	1 Tbsp. ground black pepper
½ tsp. coriander	1 cup cold water

Combine all ingredients, mix well and stuff into sheep casing or make into patties.

AMERICAN

American Farm Style Sausage

3 lbs. medium ground pork butt	1 tsp. ground cloves
2 lbs. medium ground veal	1 tsp. ground mace
1 Tbsp. salt	1 tsp. ground sage
1 Tbsp. pepper	½ cup fine dry bread crumbs
1 tsp. ground nutmeg	1 cup water

Mix all ingredients together and stuff into sheep casing or make into patties.

5 lbs. medium ground pork butt	5 tsp. salt
1 tsp. cayenne	5 tsp. black pepper
1 Tbsp. thyme	1 cup cold water

Combine all ingredients, mix well and stuff into sheep casing.

5 lbs. medium ground pork butt	1 tsp. bay leaf
1 tsp. thyme	2 tsp. black pepper
1 tsp. coriander	2 Tbsp. salt
1 tsp. marjoram	1 cup water

Combine all ingredients, mix well and stuff into sheep casing or make patties.

5 lbs. coarse ground pork butt	1 tsp. cayenne
1½ tsp. thyme	1 Tbsp. black pepper
1½ tsp. basil	1 Tbsp. salt
1½ tsp. sage	1 cup chopped parsley
	1 cup cold water

Combine all ingredients, mix well and stuff into sheep casing. To cook, fry slowly.

5 lbs. medium ground pork
   butt
1 Tbsp. powdered sage
2 tsp. summer savory
3 tsp. marjoram

1 tsp. nutmeg
1 Tbsp. salt
1 Tbsp. black pepper
1 cup cold water

Combine all ingredients, mix well and stuff into sheep casing. To cook, fry slowly.

5 lbs. medium ground pork
   butt
1½ cups finely chopped onions
5 cloves pressed garlic
½ cup chopped parsley
¼ cup sage
1 Tbsp. marjoram

1 Tbsp. cayenne
1 Tbsp. thyme
1 Tbsp. basil
1½ Tbsp. salt
1 Tbsp. black pepper
¼ lb. butter
1 cup cold water

Combine all ingredients, mix well and stuff into sheep casing, or make into patties. To cook, fry.

5 lbs. medium ground pork
   butt
1½ Tbsp. salt
1½ Tbsp. black pepper
1½ tsp. cinnamon

1 tsp. cayenne
1 tsp. nutmeg
½ cup sage
1 cup water

Combine all ingredients, mix well and stuff into sheep casing, or make into patties. To cook, fry.

AMERICAN

American Pennsylvania Dutch Sausage

5 lbs. coarse ground pork	3 Tbsp. coriander
butt	2 Tbsp. salt
⅓ cup sage	1 Tbsp. black pepper
2 Tbsp. ground cloves	1 cup cold water

Combine all ingredients, mix well and stuff into sheep casing. To cook, fry or bake.

AMERICAN

American Pig's Liver Sausage

2½ lbs. fine ground cooked	5 Tbsp. spiced salt
pork butt (boiled)	1 cup water used to boil meat
2½ lbs. fine ground cooked	1 cup finely chopped onions
pork liver (boiled)	2 Tbsp. salt

Boil pork butt and liver in water to which spiced salt has been added. (Water should cover meat.) Combine all ingredients, mix until smooth and pasty, and stuff into hog casing. Simmer in salted water for 20 minutes. Refrigerate for 24 hours. To cook, broil or fry in butter.

3 lbs. medium ground pork butt	½ tsp. nutmeg
2 lbs. mashed cooked pig's liver	½ tsp. cinnamon
2 Tbsp. salt	1 cup sauteed onion
1 Tbsp. black pepper	1 cup water

Combine all ingredients, mix well and stuff into hog casing. Tie at 4- to 5-inch intervals. To cook, fry, broil or grill.

AMERICAN

American Pork Sausage

5 lbs. medium ground pork	2 tsp. ground mace
1 Tbsp. salt	2 tsp. coriander
2 Tbsp. sage	1 whole nutmeg, grated
2 tsp. freshly ground pepper	1 cup water
1 tsp. ground cloves	

Combine all ingredients, mix well and stuff into sheep casing or make into patties.

AMERICAN

Beef Sausage

5 lbs. medium ground beef
   chuck
2 tsp. white pepper
2 tsp. ground nutmeg
2 tsp. sage

2 Tbsp. sugar
4 cloves pressed garlic
2 Tbsp. salt
1 cup water

Combine all ingredients, mix well and stuff into sheep casing. To cook, bake, broil or fry.

AMERICAN

Creole Sausage (Chaurice)

5 lbs. coarse ground pork butt
1 cup grated onions
8 cloves pressed garlic
1 Tbsp. dried hot crushed
   peppers
3 tsp. cayenne

2 tsp. black pepper
1 tsp. allspice
2 tsp. sugar
1 Tbsp. salt
1 cup chopped parsley
1 cup cold water

Combine all ingredients, mix well and stuff into hog casing. To cook, broil, bake or fry.

AMERICAN

Cuckolds

Deer stomach	*8 oz. venison*
3 oz. suet	*3 oz. oatmeal*
1 onion	*salt & pepper*

Mix above ingredients. Wash deer stomach and turn inside out. Fill the stomach with mixture, then tie at both ends. Boil for 45 minutes. When you are ready to eat this unusual sausage, fry it in hot fat until brown, about 15 minutes. Serve piping hot.

AMERICAN

Ginger Pork Sausage

5 lbs. medium ground pork butt	*3 tsp. black pepper*
5 tsp. salt	*2 tsp. ground ginger*

Combine all ingredients, mix well and stuff into hog casing. To cook, pan-fry.

AMERICAN

Louisiana Sausage

5 lbs. medium ground pork
 butt
5 tsp. salt
2 tsp. black pepper
½ tsp. allspice
2 tsp. thyme

1½ tsp. cayenne
1½ tsp. chili pepper
1 large minced onion
4 cloves pressed garlic
1 cup cold water

Combine all ingredients, mix well and stuff into hog casing or make patties.

AMERICAN

Norfolk Sausage

5 lbs. medium ground beef
 chuck
1½ Tbsp. salt
2 cups grated parmesan
 cheese
1½ Tbsp. black pepper

1 Tbsp. basil
1 Tbsp. oregano
3 tsp. mustard seed
8 cloves pressed garlic
1 small grated onion
1½ cups red wine

Combine all ingredients, mix well and stuff into hog casing. To cook, bake or broil (also, barbecue slowly).

AMERICAN

Pork Sausage (Creole-style)

5 lbs. medium ground pork	2 tsp. paprika
2 chopped large onions	½ tsp. cayenne
1 clove garlic, minced	2 Tbsp. parsley, chopped
3 tsp. salt	¼ tsp. ground allspice
2 tsp. freshly ground pepper	¼ tsp. thyme
1 tsp. crushed, dried chili pepper	1½ cups water

Combine all ingredients, mix well and stuff into sheep casing. Refrigerate. To cook, pan-fry over medium heat until brown on all sides and cook until well done.

AMERICAN

Pork Sausage

5 lbs. medium ground pork	½ cup ground sage
1 Tbsp. freshly ground black pepper	2 Tbsp. salt
	1 cup water

Combine all ingredients, mix well and stuff into hog casing. Smoke sausages until skin seems dry and hard. Hang sausage in dry place until ready to use. To cook, slice sausages down middle, lengthwise, and broil slowly, browning both sides until well done.

5 lbs. *medium ground pork*
2¼ tsp. *freshly ground black*
    pepper
2¼ tsp. *sage*

4¼ tsp. *salt*
1 cup *water*

Combine all ingredients, mix well and stuff into hog casing. To cook, use cold skillet to begin with, cover and brown well on all sides. Will keep in refrigerator for 4 weeks.

5 lbs. *medium ground pork*
1 tsp. *cayenne*
2 Tbsp. *salt*
1 cup *water*

1 Tbsp. *freshly ground black*
    pepper
1 Tbsp. *crushed sage*

Combine all ingredients, mix well and stuff into hog casing. To cook, pan-fry these sausages, beginning with cold skillet over medium heat, until well browned.

AMERICAN

Pork and Veal Sausage

4 lbs. *medium ground pork*
   butt
1 lb. *medium ground veal*
2 cups *bread crumbs*
3 Tbsp. *salt*

1½ Tbsp. *ground allspice*
1 tsp. *thyme*
1 tsp. *sage*
1½ tsp. *black pepper*
1 cup *water*

Combine all ingredients, mix well and stuff into hog or sheep casing. To cook, fry in hot fat.

AMERICAN

Rosemary Sausage

1½ lbs. *fine ground veal*
2 lbs. *fine ground pork butt*
1½ lbs. *fine ground beef chuck*
2 tsp. *black pepper*
1½ Tbsp. *salt*

1 Tbsp. *rosemary*
1 tsp. *nutmeg*
1 tsp. *thyme*
1 tsp. *marjoram*
1 cup *water*

Combine all ingredients, mix well and stuff into hog casing. Bake, fry or broil.

5 lbs. coarse ground pork butt	2½ tsp. sage
1 Tbsp. salt	6 cloves pressed garlic
1 tsp. black pepper	1 Tbsp. dried rosemary
	1 cup cold water

Combine all ingredients, mix thoroughly and stuff into hog casing. To cook, fry slowly.

AMERICAN

Spicy Pork and Veal Sausage

4 lbs. fine ground pork butt	1½ tsp. white pepper
1 lb. fine ground veal	2 Tbsp. sugar
1 cup potato flour	½ tsp. ground cloves
4 cups water	½ tsp. ground ginger
2 Tbsp. salt	

Combine all ingredients, mix well and stuff into hog casing. Sprinkle with equal parts salt and sugar. Refrigerate at least 24 hours. Poach about 20 minutes, then broil or fry.

AMERICAN

Venison Sausage

4 lbs. coarse ground venison
1 lb. fine ground bacon
1 Tbsp. salt
1 Tbsp. sage
1 tsp. allspice
2 Tbsp. sugar

1 tsp. coriander
1½ tsp. mustard seed
6 cloves pressed garlic
2 Tbsp. black pepper
1 cup cold water

Combine all ingredients, mix thoroughly and stuff into hog casing. To cook, boil, bake or fry.

3 lbs. medium ground
   venison
2 lbs. medium ground pork
   butt
1½ Tbsp. salt
1 Tbsp. black pepper

3 tsp. sugar
1 Tbsp. ground sage
4 cloves pressed garlic
1 cup water

Combine all ingredients, mix well and stuff into hog casing. To cook, bake, broil or fry.

4 lbs. medium ground venison,
   marinated*
1 lb. medium ground pork butt
1 tsp. mace
1 tsp. cumin

1 tsp. dry mustard
1 Tbsp. salt
2 cloves pressed garlic
1 cup cold water

Combine all ingredients, mix well and stuff into hog casing. To cook, broil, bake or fry.

*Marinade: 3 cups red wine   1 Tbsp. sage
           1 cup wine vinegar   1 chopped carrot
           2 bay leaves   1 large onion
           15 peppercorns

Marinate venison 3–4 days.

3 lbs. coarse ground venison   2 tsp. black pepper
2 lbs. medium ground pork   1 tsp. marjoram
   butt   4 cloves pressed garlic
2 Tbsp. salt   1 cup water
2 tsp. sugar

Combine all ingredients, mix well and stuff into hog casing. To cook, bake, broil or fry.

2½ lbs. coarse ground venison   1 Tbsp. black pepper
2½ lbs. coarse ground pork   ¼ tsp. sage
   butt   4 cloves pressed garlic
   1 Tbsp. salt   1 cup water

Combine all ingredients, mix well and stuff into hog casing. To cook, bake, broil or fry.

4 lbs. *medium ground venison*   1½ tsp. *cayenne pepper*
1 lb. *medium ground pork butt*   4 *cloves pressed garlic*
2 tsp. *sage*   1 Tbsp. *grated lemon rind*
1 Tbsp. *salt*   1 *cup water*
2 tsp. *black pepper*

Combine all ingredients, mix well and stuff into hog casing. To cook, bake, broil or fry.

3½ lbs. *fine ground venison*   3 tsp. *black pepper*
1½ lbs. *fine ground bacon*   ¾ tsp. *allspice*
4 *cloves pressed garlic*   1 tsp. *grated lemon rind*
2 tsp. *sage*   1 *cup water*

Combine all ingredients, mix well and stuff into hog casing. To cook, bake, broil or fry.

3 lbs. *fine ground venison*   1 tsp. *thyme*
1 lb. *fine ground pork butt*   ½ tsp. *nutmeg*
1 lb. *fine ground beef fat*   ½ tsp. *cayenne pepper*
1 Tbsp. *salt*   2 *bay leaves, crushed*
1 Tbsp. *black pepper*   1 *cup water*
2 tsp. *sage*

Combine all ingredients, mix well and stuff into hog casing. To cook, bake, broil or fry.

2½ lbs. coarse ground venison
2½ lbs. medium ground pork
    butt
1½ Tbsp. salt

1 Tbsp. black pepper
½ tsp. cayenne pepper
¼ tsp. ground sage
1 cup cold water

Combine all ingredients, mix well and stuff into hog casing. To cook, bake, broil or fry.

4 lbs. medium ground
    venison
1 lb. medium ground pork
    butt
1 Tbsp. salt
1 tsp. ground sage

½ tsp. ground allspice
½ tsp. cayenne pepper
¼ tsp. ground thyme
2 Tbsp. liquid smoke
6 cloves pressed garlic
1 cup cold water

Combine all ingredients, mix well and stuff into hog casing. To cook, bake, broil or fry.

2½ lbs. fine ground venison
2½ lbs. fine ground pork butt
¼ lb. butter
1 Tbsp. salt
3 tsp. black pepper

1 tsp. cayenne pepper
6 cloves pressed garlic
¼ tsp. ground sage
1 cup water

Combine all ingredients, mix well and stuff into hog casing. To cook, bake, broil or fry.

4 lbs. medium ground venison
1 lb. medium ground pork butt
1 Tbsp. salt
1 tsp. sugar

3 tsp. black pepper
½ tsp. ground ginger
1 cup water

Combine all ingredients, mix well and stuff into hog casing. To cook, bake, broil or fry.

AMERICAN

Armenian Lamb Sausage

5 lbs. medium ground lamb
1 cup finely chopped onion
8 cloves pressed garlic
2 tsp. black pepper

1 Tbsp. salt
⅔ cup fresh mint leaves
1 cup water

Combine all ingredients, mix well and stuff into sheep casing. To cook, broil or barbecue.

ARMENIAN

Vienna Sausage

3½ lbs. fine ground pork butt
2½ lbs. fine ground beef stew
  meat
¼ cup fine chopped onions
2 tsp. sugar
1 tsp. cayenne

2 tsp. paprika
1 tsp. ground mace
1 Tbsp. ground coriander
1½ Tbsp. salt
¼ cup arrow root
1½ cups milk

Combine all ingredients, mix well and put through the fine blade of the grinder again. Stuff into sheep casing. Do not separate links. Place in hot water and simmer approximately 45 minutes. Remove, cool and store.

AUSTRIAN

Bavarian Bockwurst

3 lbs. fine ground veal
2 lbs. fine ground pork butt
1½ cups cream
⅓ cup chopped chives
1 cup grated onion

1½ Tbsp. white pepper
1 Tbsp. salt
¾ tsp. nutmeg
½ tsp. mace
1 cup water

Combine all ingredients, mix well and stuff into hog casing. Simmer 20 minutes, then fry.

BAVARIAN-GERMAN

Chinese Cantonese Sausage

5 lbs. coarse ground pork butt
1 Tbsp. salt
½ cup honey
¼ cup orange juice

2 Tbsp. white vinegar
1 cup soy sauce
1 cup rice wine

Combine all ingredients, mix well and stuff into hog casing. To cook, fry in peanut oil.

CHINESE

Cuban Sausage

5 lbs. coarse ground pork butt
1½ Tbsp. salt
1 Tbsp. black pepper
8 cloves pressed garlic

2 tsp. cumin
3 tsp. oregano
¾ cup annatto or paprika
2 cups water

Combine all ingredients, mix well and stuff into hog casing. To cook, barbecue, broil or fry.

CUBAN

Danish Liverwurst

4 lbs. fine ground cooked
   pork liver (boiled)
1 lb. fine ground bacon
2 cups minced onions
1½ cups milk
1½ cups evaporated milk

½ cup potato flour
6 beaten eggs
3 tsp. black pepper
2 Tbsp. salt
1 tsp. ground cloves
1 tsp. allspice

Make a sauce of the milk and potato flour, and cook until thick. Combine all ingredients, mix until smooth and pasty, and stuff into hog casing. Simmer in salted water for approximately 20 minutes. Refrigerate for 24 hours before using. Split sausage and use like a spread.

3 lbs. fine ground cooked pork
   liver (boiled)
2 lbs. fine ground cooked pork
   butt (boiled)
6 beaten eggs
1 cup onions
⅓ cup potato flour

¼ lb. butter
2½ tsp. pepper
2 Tbsp. salt
1½ tsp. allspice
1 tsp. ground cloves
3 cups milk

Make a sauce of the milk, butter and flour. Cook until thick. Combine all ingredients, mix until smooth and pasty, and stuff into hog casing. Simmer in salted water for approximately 20 minutes. Refrigerate for 24 hours before using. Split sausage and use like a spread.

DANISH

Danish Pork Sausage

5 lbs. fine ground pork butt	¼ tsp. cloves
5 tsp. salt	1 tsp. cardamom
¼ tsp. allspice	1 large minced onion
2 tsp. white pepper	1 cup cold beef bouillon

Combine all ingredients, mix well and stuff into hog casing.

DANISH

Oxford Horns

5 lbs. coarse ground pork butt	1½ tsp. nutmeg
1½ Tbsp. sage	4 tsp. salt
1½ tsp. thyme	2 tsp. black pepper
1½ tsp. marjoram	3 eggs
1 whole grated lemon peel	1 cup water

Combine all ingredients, mix well and stuff into hog casing. To cook, pan-fry or broil.

ENGLISH

Oxford Sausages

2 lbs. *fine ground pork butt*	1 tsp. *savory*
2 lbs. *fine ground veal*	1 tsp. *rosemary*
1 lb. *fine ground beef chuck*	1 *whole nutmeg, grated*
½ *loaf fresh sourdough bread*	4 tsp. *salt*
crumbs	2 tsp. *salt*
1½ *whole grated lemon peel*	2 tsp. *black pepper*
1 tsp. *thyme*	1 *cup water*
1 tsp. *sage*	4 *eggs*

Combine all ingredients, mix well and stuff into hog casing. To cook, pan-fry or broil.

ENGLISH

Quatre-Épices

This is a blend of four spices that is exclusively used in making French sausage. It consists of seven parts of white pepper mixed with one part each of ground nutmeg, cloves, cinnamon and ginger. The blend should be thoroughly mixed and stored in a tightly covered jar or plastic bag.

FRENCH

Boudins Blanc: How to Prepare

Combine all ingredients, mix well and stuff into hog casing (but not too tightly or they will burst in cooking). Tie off the casing every 6 inches with cotton string. Make a mixture of two parts water to one part milk. Bring this mixture to a boil and lower the sausage into it. It's best if you have a french fry potato basket or something similar. Keep the temperature just below boiling and cook for thirty minutes. Cool and refrigerate the sausage. To cook, fry gently in butter or grill.

Boudin Blanc De Paris

2½ lbs. fine ground pork butt
2½ lbs. fine ground chicken
    breast
  2 Tbsp. salt
2½ tsp. white pepper

1 tsp. quatre-épices
6 cups finely chopped onions
1½ cups bread crumbs soaked
    in 1 cup hot cream
8 eggs

Boudin Blanc Du Mans

5 lbs. fine ground pork butt
2 Tbsp. salt
3 tsp. quatre-épices
1½ cups finely chopped onions

¾ cup chopped parsley
2 cups cream
4 eggs

Boudin Blanc I

2½ lbs. *fine ground pork butt*
2½ lbs. *fine ground chicken*
    breast
  2 Tbsp. *salt*
  3 tsp. *white pepper*
  3 tsp. *quatre-épices*

20 *eggs*
  6 Tbsp. *rice flour and*
  6 *cups milk, mixed*
    together—avoid
    lumps

Boudin Blanc II

1 lb. *fine ground pork butt*
2 lbs. *fine ground chicken*
    breast
2 lbs. *fine ground veal*
2 Tbsp. *salt*

  2 tsp. *quatre-épices*
  2 Tbsp. *chopped parsley*
  3 *cups finely chopped onions*
12 *eggs*
  2 *cups cream*

Boudin Blanc III

2½ lbs. fine ground pork butt
2½ lbs. fine ground chicken
   breast
  2 cups sauteed onions
  2 crushed bay leaves

½ tsp. thyme
2 Tbsp. salt
2 tsp. quatre-épices
10 eggs
  6 cups scalded milk, chilled

Boudin Blanc IV

4 lbs. fine ground pork butt
1 lb. fine ground chicken liver
5 eggs
1 cup sauteed onions in butter

1½ cups cream
1½ Tbsp. salt
  1 tsp. white pepper
  ½ tsp. ground allspice

Combine all ingredients, mix well and stuff into hog casing.
Poach in boiling water for 15 minutes and fry or broil.

FRENCH

Boudin Noir

2 *lbs. coarse ground cooked pork butt*	2 *tsp. cayenne*
3 *pints hog or beef blood**	4 *cloves pressed garlic*
2 *cups fried onions*	½ *tsp. ground allspice*
1 *Tbsp. salt*	½ *tsp. ground mace*
2 *tsp. black pepper*	½ *tsp. ground cloves*
	½ *tsp. ground nutmeg*

Combine all ingredients, mix well and stuff into hog casing. To cook, place sausage in tepid water and simmer for 15 minutes. Also, you can bake it. *Add one tsp. vinegar to one qt. fresh blood to prevent it from coagulating.

1½ *cups chopped onion*	½ *tsp. freshly ground black pepper*
2 *lbs. pork fat*	
⅔ *cup cream*	½ *tsp. thyme*
4 *Tbsp. lard*	½ *tsp. bay leaf*
4 *eggs, beaten*	4 *cups fresh pork blood**

Saute onion in lard until just soft. Add pork fat and let cool. Put this in bowl and mix in cream, pepper, thyme, bay leaf and eggs. After you have mixed this well, add pork blood. Stuff the hog casing loosely. Place sausage into wire basket and cook for 20 minutes. Prick the sausages with a needle as they rise to the surface to release air, otherwise they might burst. To serve, split lengthwise and broil slowly under low heat until brown on both sides. You may also fry them if you like. *Add one tsp. of vinegar to one qt. of fresh blood to prevent coagulating.

FRENCH

Cervelat

4 lbs. medium ground pork butt	1½ Tbsp. salt
1 lb. fine ground bacon	1 tsp. thyme
1 cup chopped parsley	1 tsp. basil
¼ cup chopped scallions and greens	6 cloves pressed garlic
	1 cup dry white wine

Combine all ingredients and stuff into casing. Hang for 3–4 days in a cool place. Cook this sausage in beef bouillon for at least three hours with salt, black pepper, thyme, basil, bay leaf, parsley and chopped scallions.

FRENCH

Chicken Sausage

4 lbs. medium ground cooked white chicken	1 Tbsp. salt
1 lb. medium ground cooked bacon	1 tsp. nutmeg
	1 tsp. ground cloves
1 lb. medium ground cooked chicken livers	2 tsp. white pepper
	1 cup chicken bouillon
10 medium eggs	1 cup bread crumbs

Combine all ingredients, mix well and stuff into sheep casing. To cook, broil, bake or fry in butter.

FRENCH

French Country Beef Sausage

4 lbs. lean beef
2 lbs. lean bacon
2½ Tbsp. salt
3 tsp. freshly ground pepper

4 cloves pressed garlic
2 Tbsp. pimento, chopped
1 cup water

Grind beef with fine plate of grinder along with the bacon. Mix well with other ingredients and stuff into sheep casing. You may tie every 4–6 inches. Dry in warm oven or smoke very lightly. To serve, poach in boiling water or beef stock for about 10–12 minutes.

FRENCH

French Sausage

2 lbs. fine ground veal
2 lbs. fine ground pork
1 lb. fine ground beef
4 cloves garlic, pressed
1 large minced onion

1 cup finely chopped parsley
5 tsp. salt
2 tsp. pepper
1 cup California brandy

Combine all ingredients, mix well and stuff into hog casing.

Sprinkle with equal parts salt and brown sugar. Refrigerate at least overnight. Scald to cook and fry.

FRENCH

French Style Chorizo

5 lbs. coarse ground pork butt	1 tsp. quatre-épices
2 Tbsp. salt	2 tsp. cayenne pepper
1 tsp. sugar	4 large cloves pressed garlic
2 chopped large sweet peppers	1 cup red wine

Combine all ingredients, mix well and stuff into hog casing. Tie every 6 inches. Cool smoke lightly for 8–10 hours. To cook, fry or grill.

FRENCH

French Garlic Sausage

5 lbs. medium ground pork butt	½ tsp. cloves
	½ tsp. cinnamon
1½ Tbsp. salt	8 cloves pressed garlic
1½ tsp. black pepper	¼ cup brandy
½ tsp. cayenne	1 cup water
½ tsp. nutmeg	

Combine all ingredients, mix well and stuff into hog casing. To cook, broil or fry.

3 lbs. medium ground pork
  butt
2 lbs. medium ground beef
  chuck
1½ Tbsp. salt

3 tsp. sugar
2 tsp. white pepper
8 cloves pressed garlic
4 Tbsp. liquid smoke

Combine all ingredients, mix well and stuff into hog casing. To cook, bake or fry.

5 lbs. fine ground pork butt
1 Tbsp. sugar
8 cloves pressed garlic
1 tsp. white pepper
2 Tbsp. salt
¼ tsp. nutmeg

¼ tsp. cinnamon
¼ tsp. ginger
¼ tsp. allspice
¼ tsp. ground thyme
1 cup white wine

Combine all ingredients, mix well and stuff into hog casing. Air dry in the refrigerator 2 or 3 days. Boil this sausage or bake.

FRENCH

Saucisses D'Alsace–Lorraine

5 lbs. medium ground pork
   butt
2 Tbsp. salt
¼ tsp. ground ginger
1 tsp. sugar

1 tsp. black pepper
1 tsp. quatre-épices
1 cup white wine
3 cups finely chopped
   mushrooms

Combine all ingredients, mix well and stuff into sheep casing. Tie off into four-inch lengths. To cook, fry in butter.

FRENCH

Saucisses Cervelas

3 lbs. medium ground pork
   butt
1 lb. medium ground beef
   chuck
1 lb. fine ground bacon

2 Tbsp. salt
1 Tbsp. black pepper
8 cloves pressed garlic
1 large onion, minced
1 cup water

Combine all ingredients, mix well and stuff into hog casing. Tie every 6 or 10 inches. It can be smoked if you like. To cook, simmer in hot water or red wine.

FRENCH

Saucisses De Champagne

5 lbs. coarse ground pork butt	1 tsp. thyme
2 Tbsp. salt	1 cup chopped parsley
2 tsp. sugar	½ cup pimentos
2 tsp. black pepper	4 cloves pressed garlic
2 tsp. quatre-épices	1 cup red wine

Combine all ingredients, mix well and stuff into large sheep casing. Tie every 6 inches. Poach the sausage in simmering water for 15–20 minutes, then fry in butter or grill.

FRENCH

Saucisses Au Champagne

5 lbs. fine ground pork butt	3 cups finely chopped
2 Tbsp. salt	mushrooms
2½ tsp. quatre-épices	1 bottle champagne
6 fresh eggs	

Combine all ingredients, mix well and stuff into large sheep casing. Tie every 6 inches. Poach the sausage in simmering water for 15–20 minutes, then fry in butter or grill.

FRENCH

Saucisses Cuit Au Madère

5 lbs. fine ground pork butt	2 cups chopped mushrooms
2 Tbsp. salt	4 oz. pistachio nuts, chopped
1½ tsp. quatre-épices	1 cup Madeira wine

Combine all ingredients, mix well and stuff into hog casing. Tie every 6 inches. Simmer for 1 hour, cool and store in the refrigerator. To cook, bake.

FRENCH

Saucisses Au Cumin

2½ lbs. medium ground pork butt	1 Tbsp. black pepper
	2 Tbsp. chopped peppers
2½ lbs. fine ground beef chuck	4 Tbsp. ground cumin
4 Tbsp. salt	1 cup water
10 cloves pressed garlic	

Combine all ingredients, mix well and stuff into hog casing. Tie every 5 inches. Cool smoke for 48 hours. Dry another 5 days. To cook, fry, grill or boil.

FRENCH

Saucisses Espagnoles

5 lbs. medium ground pork
   butt
2 Tbsp. salt
3 Tbsp. sweet red pepper,
   crushed

3 tsp. quatre-épices
2 tsp. cayenne pepper
1 cup raisins, chopped
1 cup red wine

Combine all ingredients, mix well and stuff into hog casing. Tie every 5 inches. Cool smoke for 8–12 hours. To cook, fry or grill.

FRENCH

Method to Prepare Saucisses De France

Combine all ingredients, mix well and stuff into sheep casing. Tie 4–6 inches. To cook, fry in butter or grill.

Saucisses De France I

5 lbs. medium ground pork
   butt
2 Tbsp. salt
2 tsp. quatre-épices
2 tsp. black pepper

1 cup chopped parsley
1 tsp. sage
1 tsp. thyme
1 cup white wine

Saucisses De France II

2 lbs. medium ground pork butt	2 tsp. quatre-épices
1½ lbs. medium ground veal	1 cup chopped parsley
1½ lb. chopped bacon	1 cup white wine
2 Tbsp. salt	

Saucisses De France III

2 lbs. fine ground pork butt	2 tsp. quatre-épices
1½ lbs. medium ground chicken breast	1 tsp. black pepper
1½ lbs. medium ground veal	1 cup chopped parsley
2 Tbsp. salt	1 tsp. thyme
	1 cup white wine

Saucisses De France IV

5 lbs. fine ground pork butt	3 cups diced mushroom
2¼ Tbsp. spiced salt*	1 cup water
5 eggs	

Combine all ingredients, mix well and stuff into hog casing. To cook, pan fry or broil.

*Spiced Salt

7 Tbsp. salt	8 Tbsp. ground mixed spices
2½ Tbsp. black pepper	(commercial product)

Saucisses De France (Spicy)

3½ lbs. fine ground pork	¾ tsp. coriander
1½ lbs. firm bacon fat, diced	¾ tsp. marjoram
1½ Tbsp. salt	1½ tsp. thyme
2 tsp. freshly ground pepper	1 ground bay leaf
¾ tsp. savory	1 cup red wine

Combine all ingredients, mix well and stuff into sheep casing. Tie or twist into about 3-inch intervals. Dry links in a warm oven. To cook, put into boiling water and simmer for about 8 minutes. You may also pan-fry these sausages.

5 lbs. medium ground pork
   butt
1½ Tbsp. salt
½ tsp. ginger
½ tsp. nutmeg

3 tsp. sugar
2 tsp. black pepper
½ tsp. cinnamon
½ tsp. cloves
1 cup water

Combine all ingredients, mix well and stuff into sheep casing. To cook, fry in butter.

5 lbs. coarse ground pork
   butt
1½ Tbsp. salt
1 Tbsp. finely chopped
   pimento

3½ tsp. black pepper
1 Tbsp. paprika
⅛ lb. butter
1 cup cold water

Combine all ingredients, mix well and stuff into hog casing. To cook, bake or fry.

FRENCH

Saucisses Au Foir De Porc

3 lbs. medium ground pork
    butt
2 lbs. mashed pork liver
1 lb. sauteed chopped onions

2 Tbsp. salt
2 tsp. black pepper
2 tsp. quatre-épices
1 cup Kirschwasser or brandy

Combine all ingredients, mix well and stuff into hog casing. Tie off every 4–6 inches. Poach for an hour, then cool. To cook, fry or grill.

FRENCH

Saucisses Du Perigord

5 lbs. medium ground pork
    butt
2 Tbsp. salt
2 cups chopped mushrooms or
    truffles

2 tsp. sugar
2 tsp. black pepper
2 tsp. quatre-épices
1 cup white wine

Combine all ingredients, mix well and stuff into sheep casing. Tie off every 5 inches. To cook, fry in butter.

FRENCH

Saucisses De Toulouse

5 lbs. coarse ground pork butt
2 Tbsp. salt
3 Tbsp. sugar

1 tsp. quatre-épices
1 cup water

Combine all ingredients, mix well and stuff into hog casing. Tie off every 6–8 inches. To cook, fry or grill.

FRENCH

Saucisses Viennoises

2 lbs. fine ground pork butt
2 lbs. fine ground beef chuck
1 lb. fine ground veal
2 Tbsp. salt

1 tsp. quatre-épices
2 tsp. cayenne pepper
2 tsp. coriander
2 cups water

Combine all ingredients, mix well and stuff into lamb or small hog casing. Cold smoke for 8–10 hours. To cook, fry, grill or boil.

FRENCH

White Chicken Pudding

3 lbs. fine ground chicken
  breast
2 lbs. fine ground pork butt
1 cup chopped onions, sauteed
  in butter
3 bay leaves
1 tsp. thyme

5 Tbsp. salt
1 tsp. white pepper
1 tsp. mace
1 tsp. nutmeg
8 eggs
4 cups chilled scalded milk

Combine all ingredients, mix well and stuff into hog casing. To cook, simmer for 20 minutes, then broil with butter under low heat.

FRENCH

Beef Frankfurters

5 lbs. fine ground beef chuck
1 cup nonfat dry milk
3 Tbsp. coriander
1½ tsp. mace
1½ tsp. cayenne

5 cloves pressed garlic
1½ Tbsp. salt
2 tsp. sugar
⅓ cup grated onions
1 cup water

Combine all ingredients, mix well and stuff into lamb or hog casing. It's not necessary to precook these sausages. But if you decide to, bring to a boil and simmer for ten minutes. Rinse in cold water.

GERMAN

Black Pudding I

4 lbs. pork fat, cubed
4 cups onion, chopped and
    lightly sauteed in lard
4 tsp. salt
½ tsp. freshly ground black
    pepper

½ tsp. ground allspice
2 cups cream
8 cups pig's blood* (add one
    tsp. of vinegar to one qt. of
    fresh blood to prevent
    coagulating)

Mix above ingredients well. Stuff into casing rather loosely. Place puddings in wire basket or similar contraption and plunge into boiling water. Reduce heat and simmer for 20 minutes. As puddings rise to surface of water, prick skins with needle to release air. Drain and allow to cool in container. To serve, make a few slight incisions in both sides of puddings and broil slowly under low heat, making sure to brown on all sides. *For a variation of this recipe, add:

3 cloves garlic, pressed

1 lb. cooked rice or pearl barley

2 tsp. each of sage, coriander, nutmeg and rosemary (as you wish)

Black Pudding II

4 lbs. pork fat, cubed	2 cups cream
4 cups chopped onions, sauteed	8 cups pig's blood*
	3 cloves garlic, pressed
4 tsp. salt	1 lb. cooked rice
½ tsp. ground black pepper	2 tsp. each of sage, coriander,
½ tsp. ground allspice	nutmeg and rosemary

Mix above ingredients well. Stuff into casing rather loosely. Place puddings in wire basket or similar contraption and plunge into boiling water. Reduce heat and simmer for 20 minutes. As puddings rise to surface of water, prick skins with needle to release air. Drain and allow to cool in container. To serve, make a few slight incisions in both sides of puddings and broil slowly under low heat, making sure to brown on all sides. *Add one tsp. of vinegar to one qt. of fresh blood to prevent coagulating.

Black Pudding With Eggs

2 lbs. pork fat, cubed and
  slightly melted
1 cup cream
6 eggs, beaten
1 cup onion, lightly sauteed in
  fat
1 Tbsp. salt

½ tsp. freshly ground black
  pepper
½ tsp. allspice, ground
½ tsp. thyme
2 bay leaves, crushed
4 cups pig's blood*

Mix above ingredients well. Stuff into hog casing, making sure to stuff loosely as this mixture will swell when poaching. Place puddings in wire basket and put into boiling water. Reduce heat to just below boiling and cook for about 20 minutes. When the puddings rise to the surface, prick with needle to release air. To serve, split puddings and broil slowly under low heat until brown on all sides. *Add one tsp. vinegar to one qt. of fresh blood to prevent it from coagulating.

GERMAN

Blood and Tongue Sausage

9 lbs. pork back fat
3 lbs. cooked rinds
6 lbs. cooked pork tongues
2 lbs. blood*
7 oz. salt

¾ oz. pepper
½ oz. mace
¼ oz. marjoram
¼ oz. onion powder (optional)

Cube back fat and scald in boiling water. Put cooked rinds through fine plate of grinder 2 times. Cube the cooked, skinned tongues. Place blood into container of hot water to heat a little. Strain off water from pork fat and mix all ingredients together. They should be as hot as possible during the mixing procedure. Stuff into ox (preferably) casing, plunge into boiling water and reduce heat to 180° F. Cook 3–4 hours depending on size of sausages. *Add one tsp. vinegar per quart of fresh blood to keep it from coagulating.

GERMAN

Bockwurst

4½ lbs. fine ground veal
½ lb. fine ground pork fat
¾ cup finely chopped onions
3 cups milk
3 eggs

2½ tsp. ground cloves
1½ tsp. white pepper
3 tsp. finely chopped parsley
3 tsp. salt

Combine all ingredients, mix well and put through the fine blade of the grinder again. Stuff into hog casing.

3½ lbs. veal
1½ lbs. pork
3 eggs
3 cups milk

1 well-chopped large onion
3 Tbsp. parsley
3 cloves garlic
1½ tsp. pepper

Mix thoroughly the above ingredients. Grind twice and stuff into casing. Tie the sausage into links about the size of hot dogs.

Boil water and place the Bockwurst into the water. Remove from the heat and steep the sausage for 10 minutes. Fry the sausage in a skillet with butter and finely chopped onions until brown on all sides.

2½ lbs. *fine ground pork butt*	2 tsp. *mace*
2½ lbs. *fine ground veal*	1 tsp. *ground cloves*
1 Tbsp. *white pepper*	2 Tbsp. *lemon juice*
2 Tbsp. *sugar*	4 *eggs*
1 tsp. *sage*	3 *cups milk*

Combine all ingredients, mix well and stuff into hog casing. Simmer for 45 minutes. Refrigerate 24 hours before using. To cook, broil or fry in butter.

2½ lbs. *fine ground veal*	2 tsp. *white pepper*
2½ lbs. *fine ground pork butt*	¼ cup *finely chopped parsley*
2 Tbsp. *salt*	2 Tbsp. *grated lemon peel*
1 Tbsp. *sugar*	3 *eggs*
2 tsp. *mace*	1 *cup water*
1 cup *finely chopped onion*	

Combine all ingredients, mix well and stuff into sheep casing. Simmer in hot water for approximately 45–60 minutes. To cook, fry in butter. Dip in cream and broil.

GERMAN

Braunschweiger

2½ lbs. *fine ground cooked*
    pork liver (boiled)
2½ lbs. *fine ground cooked*
    pork butt (boiled)
2 Tbsp. *salt*
1 cup *grated onions*
1 Tbsp. *sugar*
2 tsp. *white pepper*

2 tsp. *ground cloves*
½ tsp. *ground ginger*
2 tsp. *ground nutmeg*
½ tsp. *ground marjoram*
¼ tsp. *sage*
¼ tsp. *allspice*
1 cup *water used for boiling*
    meat

Combine all ingredients, mix until smooth and pasty and stuff into beef, hog or cloth casing. Simmer in salted water for approximately 20 minutes. Refrigerate for 24 hours before using. This sausage is much like liverwurst. Use it as a spread.

2½ lbs. *fine ground cooked*
    pork liver (boiled)
2½ lbs. *fine ground cooked*
    pork butt (boiled)
2 Tbsp. *salt*
1 cup *grated onions*
1½ Tbsp. *ground mustard*
2 tsp. *white pepper*

½ tsp. *ground cloves*
½ tsp. *ground sage*
½ tsp. *ground ginger*
½ tsp. *ground nutmeg*
¼ tsp. *ground allspice*
¼ tsp. *marjoram*
1 cup *water used for boiling*
    meat

Combine all ingredients, mix until smooth and pasty and stuff into beef, hog or cloth casing. Simmer in salted water for approximately 20 minutes. Refrigerate for 24 hours before using. This sausage is much like liverwurst. Use it as a spread.

5 lbs. fine ground cooked pork butt (boiled)	1 Tbsp. white pepper
1½ Tbsp. salt	2 tsp. coriander
2 Tbsp. sugar	1 cup water used to boil meat

Combine all ingredients, mix until smooth and pasty and stuff into beef, hog or cloth casing. Simmer in salted water for approximately 20 minutes. Refrigerate for 24 hours before using. This sausage is much like liverwurst. Use it as a spread.

GERMAN

Bratwurst

4 lbs. fine ground pork butt	1 tsp. dried marjoram
2 lbs. fine ground veal	1½ tsp. white pepper
½ tsp. ground allspice	3 tsp. salt
1 tsp. caraway seeds	1 cup cold water

Combine all ingredients, mix well and put through the fine blade of the grinder again. Stuff into hog casing.

3 lbs. fine ground pork	2 tsp. nutmeg
2 lbs. veal	2 tsp. mace
1 Tbsp. salt	1 cup water
1 Tbsp. pepper	

Combine all ingredients. Stuff into hog casing with above mixture. Cover the Bratwurst with hot water, bring to a boil and then remove from heat. Allow sausages to stay in water until they feel firm, then drain them. Dip in milk and broil until they are golden brown on all sides.

3 lbs. medium ground pork butt	2 tsp. mace
	2 tsp. white pepper
2 lbs. medium ground veal	2 tsp. ground nutmeg
1 cup milk	½ tsp. ground ginger
2 Tbsp. salt	3 eggs

Combine all ingredients, mix well and stuff into hog casing. To cook, simmer 15 minutes (approximately), brown in butter until done, or dip in cream and broil.

5 lbs. medium ground pork butt	1 Tbsp. allspice
	1 tsp. sage
1 Tbsp. salt	1 cup water
1 Tbsp. white pepper	

Combine all ingredients, mix well and stuff into hog casing. To cook, simmer 15 minutes (approximately), brown in butter until done, or dip in cream and broil.

2½ lbs. *medium ground veal*	1 *Tbsp. salt*
2½ lbs. *medium ground pork* *butt*	3 *tsp. white pepper*
2 *tsp. mace*	1½ *cups water*
2 *tsp. nutmeg*	1 *cup milk-soaked bread* *crumbs*

Combine all ingredients, mix well and stuff into hog casing. To cook, fry in butter, dip in milk and broil or barbecue.

GERMAN

Frankfurters (Wieners/Hot Dogs)

3 lbs. *fine ground beef chuck*	1 *tsp. ground mace*
2 lbs. *fine ground pork butt*	4 *cloves pressed garlic*
2 *tsp. white pepper*	1½ *Tbsp. salt*
1 *tsp. ground coriander*	1½ *cups water*
1 *tsp. ground ginger*	

Combine all ingredients, mix well and stuff into sheep casing. Smoke for 2 or 3 hours at 115°F. or until a rich orange color is reached. Then cook in water heated to 160°–170°F. until frankfurters float. Cooking time depends on the thickness of the hot dog. I think you know the rest.

3 lbs. *fine ground beef chuck*	2 tsp. *mace*
2 lbs. *fine ground pork butt*	¼ tsp. *cayenne pepper*
1½ Tbsp. *salt*	2 cloves *pressed garlic*
1 Tbsp. *white pepper*	1½ cups *water*

Combine all ingredients, mix well and stuff into sheep casing. Smoke for 2 or 3 hours at 115°F. or until a rich orange color is reached. Then cook in water heated to 160°–170°F. until frankfurters float. Cooking time depends on the thickness of the hot dog.

3 lbs. *fine ground beef chuck*	2 tsp. *mace*
2 lbs. *fine ground pork butt*	4 cloves *pressed garlic*
2 Tbsp. *salt*	3 Tbsp. *ground mustard*
2 Tbsp. *sugar*	1½ cups *water*
1½ tsp. *white pepper*	

Combine all ingredients, mix well and stuff into sheep casing. Cook in 160°–170°F. water until the frankfurters float. Cool quickly. (If the casing splits, the water is too hot.) Can be smoked, or liquid smoke can be added.

GERMAN

Frankfurter (Wienerwurst)

3½ lbs. fine ground pork butt
1½ lbs. fine ground beef stew
 meat
¾ cup finely chopped onions
3 cloves pressed garlic
2 tsp. ground coriander
½ tsp. marjoram
½ tsp. ground mace

¾ tsp. ground mustard
2 tsp. paprika
2 tsp. white pepper
2 egg whites
1 Tbsp. sugar
1 Tbsp. salt
½ cup milk
1 cup cold water

Puree all ingredients except the meat. Mix well and put through the fine blade of the grinder again. Stuff into small hog or sheep casing. Parboil (w/o separating them) in simmering water for approximately 20 minutes. Place in ice water, remove and store.

GERMAN

Gehirnwurst

2½ lbs. coarse ground pork
2½ lbs. pork brains (cooked in
 salted, acidulated water)
2 Tbsp. salt

1 Tbsp. pepper
2 tsp. mace
1 cup water

Cook pork brains until done. Combine all ingredients, mix well and stuff into hog casing. To cook, poach in boiling water, or fry or bake.

GERMAN

Knackwurst

4 lbs. medium ground pork	1½ Tbsp. cumin
2 lbs. beef	1 Tbsp. garlic powder
3 Tbsp. salt	1 cup water

Combine all ingredients and stuff into hog casing. Dry 2 days in refrigerator, then cool smoke until the sausages turn an amber color. Poach 10 minutes, then saute in butter until nicely browned.

2 lbs. coarse ground beef chuck	1 tsp. mace
3 lbs. coarse ground pork butt	1½ Tbsp. salt
6 cloves pressed garlic	2 tsp. sugar
1 cup grated onions	1 Tbsp. black pepper
1 Tbsp. coriander	

Combine all ingredients, mix well and stuff into hog casing. Smoke if you like, or add liquid smoke (1 tsp. per lb.). To cook, bake, broil, boil or fry.

GERMAN

Konigswurst

2½ lbs. coarse ground chicken meat	2 Tbsp. salt
2½ lbs. partridge meat	2 tsp. pepper
¾ cup mushrooms, chopped	2 tsp. mace
2 eggs	1 cup Rhine wine

Combine all ingredients, mix well and put into sheep casing. To cook, pan-fry, or broil or bake until a nice golden brown on all sides.

GERMAN

Knockwurst

3 lbs. *fine ground beef chuck*	2 tsp. *mace*
2 lbs. *fine ground pork butt*	¼ tsp. *ground allspice*
2 Tbsp. *salt*	½ tsp. *coriander*
2 tsp. *sugar*	1 Tbsp. *paprika*
2½ Tbsp. *white pepper*	4 cloves *pressed garlic*
	1 cup *water*

Combine all ingredients, mix well and stuff into hog casing. To cook, bake or fry.

GERMAN

Liverwurst

2½ lbs. *fine ground cooked pork liver (boiled)*	2¼ tsp. *white pepper*
	½ tsp. *ground sage*
2½ lbs. *fine ground cooked pork butt (boiled)*	½ tsp. *marjoram*
	½ tsp. *ground nutmeg*
2 Tbsp. *salt*	¼ tsp. *ground ginger*
1 cup *grated onions*	1 cup *water used to boil meat*
1 Tbsp. *sugar*	

Combine all ingredients, mix until smooth and pasty and stuff into beef, hog or cloth casing. Simmer in salted water for approximately 20 minutes. Refrigerate for 24 hours before using. Use as a spread.

3 lbs. fine ground cooked pork liver (boiled)	1 tsp. black pepper
2 lbs. fine ground cooked pork butt (boiled)	1 tsp. allspice
	¼ tsp. thyme
1 small grated onion	¼ tsp. sage
5 tsp. salt	⅛ tsp. cayenne
	1 cup water used to boil meat

Combine all ingredients, mix until smooth and pasty and stuff into hog, beef or cloth casing. Simmer in salted water for approximately 20 minutes. Refrigerate for 24 hours before using.

4 lbs. fine ground cooked pork butt (boiled)	1 tsp. sage
	1 tsp. cayenne pepper
1 lb. fine ground cooked pork liver (boiled)	1 tsp. allspice
	1 cup water used to boil meat
3 tsp. white pepper	

Combine all ingredients, mix until smooth and pasty and stuff into beef, hog or cloth casing. Simmer in salted water for approximately 20 minutes. Refrigerate for 24 hours before using. This sausage is a spread.

2 lbs. *fine ground cooked pork*
    butt (boiled)
3 lbs. *fine ground cooked pork*
    liver (boiled)
1 *large grated onion*
1 Tbsp. *salt*

1 Tbsp. *white pepper*
1 tsp. *allspice*
¼ tsp. *thyme*
¼ tsp. *sage*
1 *cayenne pepper*
1 *cup water used to boil meat*

Combine all ingredients, mix until smooth and pasty and stuff into beef, hog or cloth casing. Simmer in salted water for approximately 20 minutes. Refrigerate for 24 hours before using. This sausage is a spread.

2 lbs. *fine ground cooked pork*
    butt (boiled)
3 lbs. *fine ground cooked pork*
    liver (boiled)
1 *medium onion, grated*
1 lb. *bacon*

1½ tsp. *salt*
1½ tsp. *white pepper*
1 tsp. *allspice*
1 *cup water used to boil*
    meat

Combine all ingredients, mix until smooth and pasty and stuff into hog, beef or cloth casing. Simmer in salted water for approximately 20 minutes. Refrigerate for 24 hours before using. This sausage is much like Mettwurst. Use it as a spread.

2½ lbs. *fine ground cooked
pork butt (boiled)*
2½ lbs. *fine ground cooked
pork liver (boiled)*
½ cup *finely chopped onions*
1 Tbsp. *salt*
1 Tbsp. *white pepper*

1 tsp. *ground ginger*
1 tsp. *ground marjoram*
¼ tsp. *ground cloves*
¼ tsp. *ground cinnamon*
4 Tbsp. *liquid smoke*
1 cup *water used to boil meat*

Combine all ingredients, mix until smooth and pasty and stuff into beef, hog or cloth casing. Simmer in salted water for approximately 20 minutes. Refrigerate for 24 hours before using. This sausage is a spread.

GERMAN

Mettwurst

3 lbs. *fine ground cooked pork
butt (boiled)*
2 lbs. *fine ground cooked pork
liver (boiled)*

1 Tbsp. *salt*
3 tsp. *white pepper*
3 tsp. *coriander*
1 cup *water used to boil meat*

Combine all ingredients, mix until smooth and pasty and stuff into hog, beef or cloth casing. Simmer in salted water for approximately 20 minutes. Refrigerate for 24 hours before using. This sausage is much like liverwurst. Use it as a spread.

GERMAN

Metz

4 lbs. fine ground beef chuck	1 tsp. ground coriander
1 lb. fine ground bacon	1 Tbsp. salt
1 Tbsp. black pepper	1 cup Rhine wine

Combine all ingredients, mix well and stuff into hog casing. Tie off in 6-inch lengths. Cold smoke for 24 hours. To cook, fry or bake.

GERMAN

Schwabischewurst

5 lbs. fine ground pork butt	6 cloves pressed garlic
2 Tbsp. salt	2 Tbsp. caraway seeds
3 tsp. black pepper	1 cup cold water
3 tsp. sugar	

Combine all ingredients, mix thoroughly and stuff into hog casing. To cook, bring to a boil and simmer approximately 40 minutes. Bake, fry or eat as is.

GERMAN

Wurstchen

3 lbs. medium ground pork
  butt
2 lbs. medium ground veal
2 Tbsp. salt

1 Tbsp. black pepper
2 Tbsp. pimento
2 tsp. cardamon
1 cup Rhine wine

Combine all ingredients, mix well and stuff into sheep casing.
Poach about 5 minutes, then broil.

GERMAN

Greek Loukanika Sausage

5 lbs. coarse ground pork butt
3 tsp. salt
7 cloves pressed garlic
1 Tbsp. thyme
1 Tbsp. marjoram

1½ tsp. ground allspice
1½ tsp. coriander
1 tsp. crushed bay leaf
1½ Tbsp. grated orange peel
1 cup red wine

Combine all ingredients, mix well and stuff into hog casing, or
make patties.

GREEK

Greek Orange Sausage

3 lbs. fine ground pork butt
2 lbs. fine ground beef
3 cloves pressed garlic
1 large orange
1 Tbsp. cinnamon

1 Tbsp. allspice
1 Tbsp. black pepper
1 Tbsp. salt
1 cup white wine

Combine orange peel, garlic, cinnamon, allspice, pepper, salt and wine. Mix in blender until the orange peel is finely chopped. Mix well into meat and stuff into hog casing, or make patties.

GREEK

Greek Pork Sausage

5 lbs. medium ground pork
    butt
1 large finely chopped onion
6 cloves pressed garlic
2 tsp. black pepper
2 tsp. oregano leaves
¾ tsp. cayenne

¾ tsp. chili powder
¾ tsp. allspice
¾ tsp. thyme
2 bay leaves
½ cup chopped parsley
1 cup water

Combine all ingredients, mix well and stuff into hog casing. To cook, bake or fry.

GREEK

Blood Sausage

5 lbs. *coarse ground cooked*
    pork butt (boiled)
2 Tbsp. *salt*
1 cup *grated onion*
1 Tbsp. *black pepper*

½ tsp. *ground marjoram*
½ tsp. *ground thyme*
½ tsp. *mace*
½ tsp. *ground cloves*
1 qt. *pork blood**

Combine all ingredients, mix well and stuff into hog casing. To cook, place sausage into tepid water and simmer for 15 minutes. You can also bake it. *Add one tsp. vinegar per quart of fresh blood to keep it from coagulating.

HUNGARIAN

Fish Sausage (Rabakozi Halkolbasz)

4 *white rolls*
2 cups *milk*
5 lbs. *fish fillet*
8 *eggs*

4 Tbsp. *parsley*
1 tsp. *pepper*
2 tsp. *salt*

Soak rolls in milk, squeeze, shred and mix the rolls with the fish, eggs, parsley, salt and pepper, and stuff in sheep casing. Fry or broil sausage.

HUNGARIAN

Hazi Kolbasz

5 lbs. medium ground pork	1½ Tbsp. paprika
4 cloves garlic	½ tsp. ground cloves
2 Tbsp. salt	1 lemon rind
2 tsp. black pepper	1 cup water

Combine all ingredients and stuff into hog casing. Bake about 1 hour at 350°F.

HUNGARIAN

Hungarian Hurka

4 lbs. pork butt	1 Tbsp. black pepper
2 lbs. pork heart	⅛ tsp. ground marjoram
1 lb. pork jowl	1 large onion fried in ¼ cup
1 lb. pork liver	lard
¼ cup salt	5 lbs. cooked rice

Cook and grind meat through coarse blade. Add 1 cup of juice from the boiled meat. Mix all together and stuff into hog casing. Drop into boiling water. Boil for 1 minute, remove and bake later.

3 lbs. coarse ground cooked
   pork butt
2 lbs. coarse ground cooked
   pork liver
2 Tbsp. salt
1 large grated fried onion

1 Tbsp. black pepper
1 tsp. marjoram
2 Tbsp. paprika
½ lb. dried rice (cooked in
   broth from meat)

Combine all ingredients, mix well and stuff into hog casing. To cook, bake.

3 lbs. coarse ground cooked
   pork butt (boiled)
2 lbs. coarse ground cooked
   beef or pork heart (boiled)
4 cups cooked rice (cooked in
   water used for cooking meat)

2 cups fried onions
1½ Tbsp. salt
2 tsp. black pepper
1 tsp. cloves
1 cup meat juice

Combine all ingredients, mix well and stuff into hog casing. To cook, place Hurka into tepid water and simmer for 15 minutes. Also, you can bake it.

HUNGARIAN

Hungarian Kolbasz

12 lbs. coarse ground pork	1 tsp. cayenne pepper
¼ cup salt	6 large cloves garlic
2 Tbsp. black pepper	1 cup water
3 Tbsp. paprika	

Cook garlic in water, then mash it. Add liquid and garlic to mixture, and mix. Stuff into hog casing.

HUNGARIAN

Majas Hurka (Hot Liver Sausage)

1 lb. pork butt	2 large onions
2 lbs. pork liver	½ lb. lard
2 lbs. pork lungs	1 Tbsp. pepper
2 Tbsp. salt	1 tsp. marjoram
1 cup uncooked rice	
2½ cups beef broth (bouillon)	

Boil pork liver and lungs together with 1 Tbsp. salt. Cook rice in beef broth and fry onions until soft. Combine all ingredients except the rice and put through the fine plate of the grinder. Add rice, mix well and stuff into hog casing. To cook, boil sausage for 10 minutes, then fry or bake.

HUNGARIAN

Irish Sausage

5 lbs. coarse ground pork butt	3 tsp. basil
5 cups bread crumbs	3 tsp. rosemary
4 eggs, lightly beaten	3 tsp. marjoram
8 cloves pressed garlic	3 tsp. black pepper
1 Tbsp. salt	2 cups water
3 tsp. thyme	

Combine all ingredients, mix well and stuff into sheep casing. To cook, fry in butter or oil.

IRISH

Bologna

3 lbs. beef chuck	½ tsp. ground ginger
2 lbs. pork butt	½ tsp. ground mustard
2 Tbsp. salt	½ tsp. ground nutmeg
1 Tbsp. white pepper	2 cups water
4 cloves pressed garlic	
½ tsp. ground coriander	

Grind beef with half of the salt in coarse grinding plate, and allow to cure in refrigerator for about 48 hours. Use the other half of the salt when putting pork through coarse grinding plate, and cure this overnight. Regrind cured beef using fine plate, then add pork and grind mixture again. Add spices and water and stir heartily until the whole mixture has become sticky. It may take you 30–40 minutes to reach this consistency. Stuff the sausage into beef casing or muslin bags and hang in a cool place overnight. Smoke at about 115°F. for 2 hours or until a rich, mahogany brown. Put the hot, freshly smoked sausage immediately into water heated to about 170°F., and cook it until it squeaks when the pressure of the thumb and finger on the casing is suddenly released. The usual cooking time for sausage stuffed in beef intestine is 15–30 minutes—for larger casing, 60–90 minutes. Plunge the cooked sausage into cold water and chill it. Hang in a cool place.

ITALIAN

More Bologna Recipes

In each case, combine all ingredients, mix well and refrigerate for 24 hours. Stuff into hog (for ring bologna) or beef (for large sausage) casing. Dry the sausage and hang in a preheated smokehouse (120°F.). Smoke for approximately 3 hours or until a rich orange color. Remove from smokehouse and boil in 170°F. water until the inside temperature of the bologna has reached 150°F. Rinse in cold water and you're ready.

4 *lbs. fine ground beef chuck*	1 *tsp. cayenne*
1 *lb. fine ground pork butt*	4 *cloves pressed garlic*
2 *Tbsp. salt*	2 *tsp. white pepper*
1 *Tbsp. paprika*	1½ *cups water*
2 *Tbsp. sage*	

3 *lbs. fine ground beef chuck*	2 *tsp. nutmeg*
2 *lbs. fine ground pork butt*	½ *tsp. allspice*
2 *Tbsp. salt*	½ *cup grated onions*
2 *tsp. white pepper*	1½ *cups water*
1 *Tbsp. paprika*	

3 lbs. fine ground beef chuck
2 lbs. fine ground pork butt
1 Tbsp. white pepper
1½ Tbsp. salt
¾ tsp. ground coriander

¾ tsp. ground ginger
¾ tsp. ground mustard
¾ tsp. ground nutmeg
4 cloves pressed garlic
1½ cups water

4 lbs. fine ground pork butt
1 lb. fine ground bacon
1½ Tbsp. salt
2 Tbsp. white pepper

1½ Tbsp. ground ginger
1 Tbsp. ground cloves
1 Tbsp. sage
1½ cups water

5 lbs. fine ground beef chuck
½ cup sugar
1½ Tbsp. salt
1½ Tbsp. black pepper

½ tsp. coriander
4 cloves pressed garlic
1½ cups water

3 lbs. fine ground beef chuck
2 lbs. fine ground pork butt
2 Tbsp. salt
1 tsp. cayenne
1½ tsp. white pepper

½ tsp. mace
½ tsp. allspice
1 cup grated onion
1½ cups water

3 lbs. *fine ground beef chuck*	½ tsp. *ground nutmeg*
2 lbs. *fine ground pork butt*	½ tsp. *savory*
1½ Tbsp. *salt*	½ tsp. *thyme*
1½ Tbsp. *sage*	2 tsp. *marjoram*
1 tsp. *cayenne*	1 cup *grated onions*
1 tsp. *black pepper*	1½ cups *water*
½ tsp. *cloves*	

4 lbs. *fine ground beef chuck*	2 Tbsp. *sugar*
1 lb. *fine ground pork butt*	1 tsp. *cayenne*
1½ Tbsp. *salt*	4 cloves *pressed garlic*
1 tsp. *coriander*	1½ cups *water*
1 Tbsp. *white pepper*	

ITALIAN

Cooked Salami

2½ lbs. *fine ground beef chuck*	3 tsp. *whole black pepper*
2½ lbs. *fine ground pork butt*	1 Tbsp. *cardamom*
3 Tbsp. *salt*	10 cloves *pressed garlic*
5 Tbsp. *honey*	1 cup *dry nonfat milk*
1 Tbsp. *black pepper*	1 cup *water*

Combine all ingredients, mix well and refrigerate for 24 hours. Stuff into cellulose or fiber casing. Cool smoke for 1–2 hours or until the casing is dry. Gradually increase the temperature of the smokehouse to 160°–165° F. Lightly smoke until an internal temperature of 140°F. is reached. Chill the sausage in cold water and hang at room temperature 2–3 hours. Refrigerate.

ITALIAN

Cotechino

5 lbs. coarse ground fresh ham with skin	2 tsp. ground cinnamon
2 Tbsp. salt	2 tsp. cayenne pepper
1⅓ Tbsp. coarse black pepper	½ cup parmesan cheese
2 tsp. ground nutmeg	1 tsp. ground cloves
	1 cup cold water

Combine all ingredients, mix well and stuff into hog casing. Allow 2 days in the refrigerator before eating or freezing.

ITALIAN

Luganega

5 lbs. fine ground pork butt	½ tsp. grated orange peel
1½ cups grated parmesan cheese	1¼ tsp. black pepper
⅔ tsp. ground nutmeg	2 cloves pressed garlic
⅔ tsp. ground coriander	1 Tbsp. salt
½ tsp. grated lemon peel	1 cup dry vermouth

Combine all ingredients, mix well and stuff into hog casing. Let stand in the refrigerator 1 or 2 days before freezing.

ITALIAN

Italian Pepper Sausage

4½ lbs. coarse ground pork	4 tsp. fennel
1½ lbs. salt pork	2 Tbsp. crushed red pepper,
1 clove garlic	dried
1 onion, quartered	¼ tsp. thyme
1½ Tbsp. freshly ground black	½ tsp. bay leaf, crushed
pepper	¼ tsp. coriander
2 Tbsp. salt	1 cup red wine
4 Tbsp. paprika	

Combine all ingredients, mix well and stuff into hog casing. You may split lengthwise and broil under medium heat, or pan-fry until brown on all sides and well done.

ITALIAN

Italian Sausage

5 lbs. coarse ground pork butt	1 Tbsp. fennel seeds
1 Tbsp. salt	1 tsp. anise seed
1 Tbsp. coarse black pepper	1 cup cold water
5 cloves pressed garlic	

Add 1 Tbsp. crushed hot pepper for hotter style sausage. Combine all ingredients, mix well and stuff into hog casing or make patties.

5 lbs. coarse ground pork butt	1 Tbsp. salt
12 cloves pressed garlic	2 tsp. black pepper
1 Tbsp. crushed red pepper	½ tsp. nutmeg
1 Tbsp. fennel seeds	½ tsp. coriander
1 tsp. thyme	1 Tbsp. paprika
2 bay leaves, crushed	1 cup cold water

Combine all ingredients, mix well and stuff into hog casing. To cook, fry or bake.

5 lbs. coarse ground pork butt	3 tsp. black pepper
1 Tbsp. salt	½ cup chopped parsley
8 cloves pressed garlic	1 tsp. thyme
2 Tbsp. oregano	1 cup grated Romano cheese
2 Tbsp. fennel seeds	1 cup water

Combine all ingredients, mix well and stuff into hog casing. To cook, fry or bake.

5 lbs. coarse ground pork butt	1 tsp. crushed hot pepper
1 Tbsp. salt	¼ cup chopped parsley
2 Tbsp. black pepper	1 cup water
1½ Tbsp. fennel seeds	

Combine all ingredients, mix well and stuff into hog casing. To cook, fry or bake.

3 lbs. coarse ground pork butt	¼ cup chopped parsley
2 lbs. coarse ground beef chuck	1 Tbsp. salt
6 cloves pressed garlic	1 Tbsp. black pepper
2 bay leaves, crushed	1 tsp. nutmeg
2 Tbsp. basil	1 tsp. thyme
	1 cup water

Combine all ingredients, mix well and stuff into hog casing. To cook, fry or bake.

ITALIAN

Italian Sausage (Hot)

5 lbs. coarse ground pork butt	1 Tbsp. crushed hot pepper
2 Tbsp. salt	½ tsp. caraway seed
2 tsp. fennel seed	2 tsp. coriander
2 tsp. sugar	1 cup water

Combine all ingredients, mix well and stuff into hog casing. To cook, fry or bake.

5 lbs. coarse ground pork butt	2 Tbsp. paprika
5 tsp. fennel seeds	1½ tsp. black pepper
5 tsp. crushed hot peppers	1 cup cold water
5 tsp. salt	

Combine ingredients, mix well and stuff into hog casing or make patties.

ITALIAN

Italian Sausage (Mild)

5 lbs. coarse ground pork
    butt
5 tsp. salt
5 tsp. fennel seeds

1½ tsp. black pepper
1½ tsp. crushed hot peppers
1 cup cold water

ITALIAN

Italian Sausage (Sweet)

5 lbs. coarse ground pork
    butt
3 tsp. fennel seed
2 tsp. white pepper

1½ tsp. sage leaves
5 cloves pressed garlic
3 tsp. salt
1 cup white wine

Combine all ingredients, mix well and stuff into hog casing or make patties.

5 lbs. coarse ground pork butt	1 tsp. black pepper
2 Tbsp. salt	2 tsp. sugar
1½ tsp. fennel seed	1 cup water

Combine all ingredients, mix well and stuff into hog casing. To cook, fry or bake.

ITALIAN

Italian Sausage (Sweet or Hot)

5 lbs. coarse ground pork butt	1⅓ Tbsp. ground coriander
1⅓ Tbsp. salt	5 cloves pressed garlic
1½ Tbsp. coarsely ground black pepper	2 Tbsp. paprika
	1 cup cold water

Add 2 tsp. crushed red peppers for hot sausage. Combine all ingredients, mix well and stuff into hog casing or make patties.

ITALIAN

Chorizo

5 lbs. coarse ground pork
   butt
½ cup red wine vinegar
1 large chopped onion
5 cloves pressed garlic
1 Tbsp. salt
3 tsp. brown sugar

1½ tsp. cumin
½ tsp. coriander
1 tsp. dried mint leaves
1 Tbsp. oregano
1 tsp. basil
3 Tbsp. chili powder
1 cup water

Combine all ingredients, mix well and stuff into hog casing.

5 lbs. coarse ground pork
   butt
2 Tbsp. salt
½ cup vinegar
2½ Tbsp. paprika

1½ crushed pepper, dried
6 cloves pressed garlic
2 tsp. oregano
1 tsp. black pepper
1 cup water

Combine all ingredients, mix well and stuff into hog casing.

5 lbs. coarse ground pork
   butt
2 Tbsp. salt
1½ tsp. cayenne pepper
½ tsp. nutmeg
½ tsp. ground ginger

2 tsp. black pepper
3 tsp. sugar
6 cloves pressed garlic
1 cup raisins
1 cup cold water

Combine all ingredients, mix thoroughly and stuff into hog casing. To cook, bake or fry.

5 lbs. coarse ground pork butt
5 cloves pressed garlic
1 cup red wine
5 Tbsp. chili pepper
4 Tbsp. paprika

2 Tbsp. oregano, crushed
1 Tbsp. ground cumin
5 tsp. salt
1 cup water

Combine all ingredients, mix well and stuff into hog casing.

MEXICAN

Sonora Chorizo

5 lbs. coarse ground pork butt
6 cloves pressed garlic
1 small diced onion
2 Tbsp. pimentos
2 Tbsp. chili powder (or more)
¼ cup brandy

¼ cup vinegar
1 tsp. black pepper
½ tsp. cinnamon
1½ tsp. cumin
1½ Tbsp. salt
1 cup water

Combine all ingredients, mix well and stuff into hog casing. If you like a little more heat in this sausage, you can add crushed red peppers or cayenne pepper. You must determine the quantity. "Fry it."

MEXICAN

Chorizo

5 lbs. coarse ground pork butt
5 tsp. salt
2 tsp. black pepper
1 Tbsp. chili powder
2 tsp. crushed hot peppers, dried

2 tsp. ground cumin
2 Tbsp. paprika
2 large minced onions
8 cloves pressed garlic
1 cup cold water

Combine all ingredients, mix well and stuff into hog casing or make patties.

5 lbs. coarse ground pork butt
4 tsp. salt
1 Tbsp. coarsely ground black pepper
1½ Tbsp. cayenne pepper

2 tsp. hot pepper, dried
5 cloves pressed garlic
2 Tbsp. wine vinegar
1 cup red wine
1 tsp. fennel seed

Combine all ingredients, mix well and stuff into hog casing or make patties.

5 lbs. coarse ground pork butt
3 tsp. salt
1 tsp. ground cumin
1 tsp. cayenne pepper
2 Tbsp. fresh oregano

8 cloves pressed garlic
1 large finely chopped onion
¼ cup crushed chili peppers
1 cup wine vinegar

Mix all together and stuff into hog casing, or make patties. Wait 24 hours before cooking.

MEXICAN/SPANISH

Lamb Sausage

5 lbs. coarse ground lamb	2 tsp. oregano
1¾ cups chopped parsley	3 tsp. cayenne
1¾ cups minced onion	3 tsp. black pepper
2 tsp. marjoram	1 Tbsp. salt
½ tsp. cumin	1 cup cold water
1½ tsp. coriander	

Combine all ingredients, mix well and stuff into sheep casing. To cook, broil, barbecue (very nice) or bake.

MOROCCAN

Norwegian Sausage

3 lbs. coarse ground beef chuck	4 medium onions, grated
2 lbs. coarse ground pork butt	1 Tbsp. black pepper
1½ Tbsp. salt	2½ tsp. nutmeg
	1 cup cold water

Combine all ingredients, mix well and stuff into hog casing. To cook, bake or fry.

NORWEGIAN

Polish Blood Sausage

2½ lbs. coarse ground pork
   butt
2 qts. pig's blood*
2½ cups cooked rice or barley
1 tsp. ginger

1½ tsp. black pepper
1½ tsp. allspice
1 Tbsp. salt
3 cloves pressed garlic
2 tsp. baking powder

Combine all ingredients, mix well and stuff into hog casing. To cook, bake at about 375°F. for 1 hour. *Add one tsp. vinegar per quart of fresh blood to keep it from coagulating.

POLISH

Polish Kielbasa

5 lbs. coarse ground pork
2 Tbsp. salt
1½ tsp. pepper

1 tsp. marjoram
3 cloves garlic, finely chopped
1 cup water

Combine all ingredients, mix well and stuff into hog casing. To cook, cover partially and simmer for 1½ hours.

3 lbs. coarse ground pork butt	1½ tsp. marjoram
2 lbs. coarse ground stew meat	1½ tsp. savory
1½ Tbsp. salt	½ tsp. ground allspice
1½ Tbsp. coarse black pepper	6 cloves pressed garlic
	2 Tbsp. paprika
	1 cup cold water

Combine all ingredients, mix well and stuff into casings. Bake at 425°F. (oven) for 45 minutes or freeze.

5 lbs. coarse ground pork butt	8 cloves pressed garlic
1 Tbsp. salt	1 Tbsp. mustard seed
1 Tbsp. black pepper	1 cup water

Combine all ingredients, mix well and stuff into hog casing. To cook, bake, broil or fry slowly.

4 lbs. coarse ground pork butt	2 tsp. sugar
1 lb. fine ground beef chuck	1 Tbsp. marjoram
1½ Tbsp. salt	½ tsp. allspice
1 Tbsp. black pepper	1 Tbsp. caraway seeds
8 cloves pressed garlic	1 cup cold water

Combine all ingredients, mix well and stuff into hog casing. To cook, bake or broil.

POLISH

Polish Kiszka

3 lbs. coarse ground cooked pork butt	½ tsp. marjoram
2 lbs. cooked buckwheat	1 Tbsp. salt
	1 Tbsp. black pepper

Combine all ingredients, mix well and stuff into hog casing. To cook, bake or as you please.

POLISH

Polish Kiszka Z Krwia

Cook together:	1 Tbsp. ground allspice
4 split pig's feet	2 Tbsp. ground marjoram
3 lbs. cubed pork butt	2½ Tbsp. salt
7 onions	2 Tbsp. black pepper
3 lbs. cubed pork liver	
5 lbs. buckwheat	1 pt. pig's blood* (add last)

Combine all ingredients and cook until done (except the blood). Cool and add the blood. Mix well and stuff into hog casing.

Bake until done. Wonderful!! *Add one tsp. vinegar per quart of fresh blood to keep it from coagulating.

POLISH

Polish Sausage

5 lbs. medium ground pork butt	1 Tbsp. black pepper
1½ Tbsp. salt	1 tsp. marjoram
1 Tbsp. sugar	4 cloves pressed garlic
	1 cup water

Combine all ingredients, mix well and stuff into hog casing. To cook, bake or fry.

3 lbs. medium ground pork butt	2 tsp. black pepper
2 lbs. medium ground beef chuck	1 Tbsp. marjoram
5 tsp. salt	6 cloves pressed garlic
	½ tsp. cayenne

Combine all ingredients, mix well and stuff into hog casing.

4 lbs. coarse ground pork butt
1 lb. coarse ground beef stew
   meat
2 Tbsp. coarsely ground pepper
1 Tbsp. marjoram leaves

8 cloves pressed garlic
¼ tsp. ground allspice
3½ tsp. salt
1 cup cold water

Combine all ingredients, mix well and stuff into hog casing or make patties.

POLISH

Smoked Polish Kielbasa

5 lbs. fine ground pork butt
3 Tbsp. salt
1 Tbsp. sugar
1 Tbsp. black pepper

8 cloves pressed garlic
1 tsp. marjoram
1 cup water

Combine all ingredients, mix well and refrigerate for 24 hours. Stuff into large hog casing. Cool smoke for 1–2 hours or until the casing is dry. Gradually increase the temperature of the smokehouse to 160°–165°F. Apply a heavy smoke until an internal temperature of 140°F. is reached. Chill the sausage in cold water and hang at room temperature 2–3 hours. They sure smell good. Refrigerate.

POLISH

Portuguese Linguisa

5 lbs. coarse ground pork butt
2 Tbsp. salt
1 Tbsp. sugar
8 cloves pressed garlic
¼ cup wine vinegar

4 Tbsp. paprika
1 Tbsp. black pepper
3 tsp. marjoram
1 cup red wine

Combine all ingredients and mix well. Stuff into hog casing. To cook, fry in Rhine wine or bake.

5 lbs. coarse ground pork butt
3 tsp. salt
8 cloves pressed garlic
2 Tbsp. hot chili peppers,
    crushed
1 Tbsp. ground coriander

1 Tbsp. paprika
½ tsp. ground cinnamon
½ tsp. cloves
½ tsp. allspice
½ cup wine vinegar
½ cup water

Combine all ingredients, mix well and stuff into hog casing or make patties.

PORTUGUESE

Romanian Beef Sausage

5 lbs. coarse ground beef chuck
5 tsp. salt
1 tsp. pepper
5 cloves pressed garlic

1 Tbsp. soda
1½ tsp. cloves
1 cup water
2 Tbsp. sugar

Combine all ingredients, mix well and stuff into hog casing.

ROMANIAN

Romanian Mititei

5 lbs. medium ground beef chuck	1 Tbsp. black pepper
8 cloves pressed garlic	1 cup chopped parsley
3 tsp. baking soda	⅔ cup olive oil
1 Tbsp. salt	1 cup warm water

Combine all ingredients, mix well and stuff into hog casing. To cook, barbecue, broil or bake.

ROMANIAN

Romanian Pork and Beef Sausage

3 lbs. medium ground pork butt	1½ Tbsp. salt
2 lbs. medium ground beef chuck	2 tsp. black pepper
	½ tsp. marjoram
6 cloves pressed garlic	½ tsp. lovage
	1 cup water

Combine all ingredients, mix well and stuff into hog casing. Broil or bake. Very nice.

ROMANIAN

Russian Sausage

5 lbs. coarse ground pork butt
2 large chopped onions
2 Tbsp. pressed garlic
1 cup fresh parsley, chopped
3 Tbsp. dill seeds

3 Tbsp. caraway seeds
1 Tbsp. black pepper
1 Tbsp. salt
2 cups water

Combine all ingredients, mix well and stuff into hog casing.
Bake at 350°F., approximately 1 hour. This is my Gram's receipe
and is it good!

RUSSIAN

Haggis (Scottish)

1 sheep's stomach
1 sheep's lungs
1 sheep's heart
1 sheep's liver
½ lb. fresh beef suet
¾ cup oatmeal

3 onions, chopped
1 tsp. salt
⅛ tsp. pepper
pinch of cayenne
¾ cup stock
1 cup whiskey

Wash stomach thoroughly, turn inside out and scald in boiling
water. Scrape with knife. Soak overnight in cold salt water.
Simmer heart, lungs, liver for 1½ hours. Cool. Toast oatmeal in
oven. Cut away gristle and pipes, and grate liver coarsely. Chop
heart and lungs and mix all ingredients together. Add more salt
and pepper if desired. Fill stomach two-thirds full. There should
be room for the oatmeal to swell. Press air from bag and sew
securely. Prick stomach several times with a needle. Boil for 3
hours uncovered. Add water as needed. Remove threads and

serve with a spoon. This is great served with mashed potatoes and Whiskey!

SCOTTISH

Boerwors (South African Sausage)

3 lbs. beef   ½ tsp. nutmeg
2 lbs. bacon   1 tsp. coriander seed
1 tsp. pepper   ¼ pint vinegar
1 tsp. salt

Coarse grind meats with seasonings, stuff into hog casing. Cook as you would any fresh sausage.

SOUTH AFRICAN

Potatis Korv

3 lbs. coarse ground beef   2½ Tbsp. salt
   chuck   1 Tbsp. white pepper
2 lbs. potatoes   2 tsp. sugar
4 medium onions, finely   3 tsp. allspice
   chopped   1 cup water

Combine all ingredients, mix well and stuff into hog casing. To cook, simmer for 1 hour (approximately).

SWEDISH

Potatis Porv (Swedish Potato Sausage)

1 lb. medium ground chuck
1½ lbs. medium ground pork
  butt
6 parboiled diced potatoes
1 large coarsely chopped
  onion
1 tsp. white pepper

3 tsp. salt
¼ tsp. ground allspice
¼ tsp. ground mace
¼ tsp. ground nutmeg
3 cloves pressed garlic
1 cup cold water

Combine all ingredients, mix well and put through the medium grinder, then stuff into hog casing. Boil sausage in chicken broth (bouillon).

2 lbs. medium ground beef
  chuck
2 lbs. medium ground pork
  butt
1 Tbsp. salt
1½ cups finely chopped onions

2 tsp. black pepper
1 tsp. ground allspice
6 cups medium ground
  potatoes
1 cup water

Combine all ingredients, mix well and stuff into hog casing. To cook, fry, bake or boil.

1½ lbs. *medium ground beef*
1½ lbs. *medium ground pork*
　　butt
7 cups *grated potatoes*
1 cup *chopped onions*

1 tsp. *ground ginger*
2 tsp. *black pepper*
3 tsp. *salt*
1 cup *water*

Combine all ingredients, mix well and stuff into hog casing. Make a mixture of 1 tsp. salt to each 2 qts. water, cover sausage and refrigerate. To cook, simmer in salted water approximately ½ hour, then fry in butter.

SWEDISH

Scandinavian Sausage

2½ lbs. *fine ground veal*
2½ lbs. *fine ground pork*
2 large *potatoes (mashed)*
6 tsp. *salt*
2 tsp. *sugar*

1 tsp. *black pepper*
1 tsp. *ground ginger*
1½ tsp. *ground allspice*
2 cups *milk*

Combine all ingredients, mix well and stuff into hog casing. Sprinkle with equal parts salt and brown sugar. Refrigerate at least overnight. To cook, hot smoke 3 or 4 hours, or scald and brown.

SWEDISH

Swiss Bauerwrst (Smoked)

3 lbs. fine ground beef chuck
2 lbs. fine ground pork butt
5 tsp. salt
5 tsp. caraway seeds

1 tsp. ground allspice
1½ cups cream
1 cup water

Combine all ingredients, mix well and stuff into hog casing. Sprinkle with equal parts salt and brown sugar. Refrigerate at least overnight. Hot smoke until done (approximately 3 hours), or bake.

SWISS

Blood Sausage

4 lbs. coarse ground cooked
    pork butt (boiled)
3 cups cooked barley (cooked in
    water used for pork)
2 Tbsp. salt

1 cup sugar
1 tsp. ginger
1 tsp. ground allspice
2 qts. pork blood*

Combine all ingredients, mix well and stuff into hog casing. To cook, place sausage into tepid water and simmer for 15 minutes. Also, you can bake it. *Add one tsp. vinegar per quart of fresh blood to keep it from coagulating.

4 lbs. coarse ground cooked
   pork butt (boiled)
1 qt. pork blood
2 cups potato flour
1 cup sugar

2 tsp. soda
1½ tsp. black pepper
1½ cup pork broth
2 Tbsp. salt

Combine pork blood and pork broth with the potato flour, and mix thoroughly. Add to the other ingredients, again mix thoroughly and stuff into hog casing. To cook, place in tepid water and simmer for 15 minutes. Also, you can bake.

YUGOSLAVIAN

Blood Sausage (Louise-style)

This recipe used by a Slovene lady from the old country who lives in Niles, Ohio where I was born. She makes huge amounts of this *fantastic* sausage and sells it to drooling local residents. I wasn't able to get the exact measurements, so you're on your own. Experiment. That's half the fun of making sausage anyway!

1 pig's head
pork butts
pig's heart
pig's lungs
pig's blood, fresh*
rice

black pepper (3 Tbsp.)
cinnamon (1 Tbsp.)
ground cloves (1 Tbsp.)
allspice (1 Tbsp.)
salt to taste (4 Tbsp.)
sweet majoram (1 Tbsp.)

All I know is that you cook all the meats together for about 3 hours or until the meat falls off the bones. Cool. Put meat through coarse plate of grinder. Cook rice (about ⅓ as much rice as meat) until just a little hard. Mix rice into meat mixture, along with rest of seasonings. Blend in blood (about one or two quarts, depending upon how much sausage you are making) and stuff loosely into casing. Boil one hour in deep kettle, being sure to prick as the sausage rises to the surface to eliminate bursting of skins. May be eaten as is, or split and broiled or pan-fried. *Add one tsp. vinegar per quart of fresh blood to keep it from coagulating.

YUGOSLAVIAN

Blood Sausage (Slovene-style)

This is a rather general recipe for you to experiment with. It's a very old one from the old country, and it was not possible for me to get the exact proportions. Good luck!

1 pig's head	*parsley*
1 small pork butt	*bay leaf*
1 pig's heart	*allspice*
rice, 50% as much as meat	*pig's blood, enough to make*
salt and pepper to taste	*loose mixture**
onion	

Boil meats in water with onion, parsley, allspice and bay leaf until meat falls off the bone (about 3 hours). Allow to cool. Put through coarse plate of grinder and add half-cooked rice and salt and pepper. Then mix in pig's blood to make a rather loose mixture. Stuff into casing loosely, as this sausage will tend to swell while cooking. Cook in boiling water until sausage swells. Prick to avoid bursting of skins. Eat as is, or broil or pan-fry until nicely browned. *Add one tsp. vinegar per quart of fresh blood to keep it from coagulating.

YUGOSLAVIAN

Yugoslavian Čevapčiči

5 lbs. medium ground beef chuck	1 cup chopped parsley
10 cloves pressed garlic	1 Tbsp. salt
1 Tbsp. paprika	1 Tbsp. black pepper
2 tsp. cayenne	1 cup water

Combine all ingredients, mix well and stuff into hog casing. To cook, barbecue, fry or broil.

YUGOSLAVIAN

Slovene Čevapčiči

5 lbs. medium ground beef chuck	1½ Tbsp. salt
juice of 8 cloves garlic	2 tsp. black pepper
1 large finely diced onion	1 cup water

Combine all ingredients, mix well and stuff into hog casing, or make into patties. To cook, barbecue or fry.

YUGOSLAVIAN

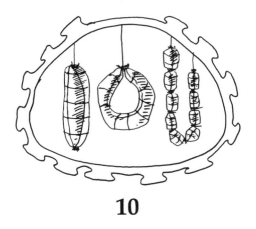

10

Dry and Semidry
Sausage Recipes

MOST OF THE recipes for dry sausages are as old as the hills. However, when you start looking for information regarding the preparation of these sausages, most everyone will tell you how difficult they are to make. Rarely will you be lucky enough to get an exact formula for preparation. The large producers of dry sausage protect their processing techniques as if they were pure gold and with good reason, I suppose!

Making Dry Sausage

When you decide to embark on the process of making dry sausage, there are some things to keep in mind. The most important is to eliminate or inhibit the growth of the bacteria known as clostridium botulinum belonging to the bacillaceae family. Sounds like a family I grew up with . . . Anyway, the end result is the same, we call it botulism. Strangely enough, botulism gets its name from a German doctor who back in 1896 was involved in a case of food poisoning caused by, of course, some bad sausage. Please read and follow the information in the section on spoilage.

Please remember to use Certified Pork for these dry sausage recipes. This is pork that has been frozen to make it trichinosis-free and should be labeled so. If you can't find Certified Pork, freeze the pork yourself as mentioned in an earlier chapter. If you decide to freeze the pork yourself, make sure your thermometer is accurate. This is nothing to play around with.

Preparing the Meat

Some types of dry sausage will not call for grinding the meat. In such cases, just cube the meat into ¾ inch squares. Add the cure and refrigerate for 3 to 4 days. Then add the rest of the seasonings and stuff into the casing. You will then be ready to proceed with the usual dry sausage instructions.

Many recipes for dry sausage and semidry sausage will call for a wide variety of meats. I would try to standardize, limiting yourself to beef and Certified Pork. Chuck roast is perfect for dry sausage. Also, Boston Butt works perfectly well.

Curing the Sausage

Most sausage is a combination of chopped or ground meat that is seasoned and stuffed into casing of one kind or another. In making dry sausage, the meat must be cured for 2 to 3 days in the refrigerator prior to stuffing it into the casing. It is of the utmost importance that the cure be mixed well into the sausage meat. Also, the cure should be mixed together a few days prior to combining it with the sausage meat to allow the seasonings to blend. The cure itself generally consists of one pound of sugar, five pounds of salt, and three tablespoons of garlic powder.

There are commercial meat cures in the marketplace all containing different proportions of salt, sugar, sodium nitrate and nitrite . . . yes, and other ingredients too. You will notice I've not included potassium nitrate, sodium nitrate, or nitrite in the recipes in this book. If you are making your own sausage, you can choose just what ingredients you want to add.

For information on commercial cures, write to: Morton's Tenderquick, Cumberland General Store, Route 3, Crossville, Tennessee 38555; or Sausage Maker, 177 Military Road, Buffalo, New York 14207.

Using the Cure

To start the curing process, dice the meat to fit into the grinder, mix well with the cure, and grind this mixture with the coarse plate. Place the mixture in a shallow pan and allow it to stay in refrigerator for 2 to 3 days. Then add the rest of the seasonings, grind again, and stuff into the casing. Hang the sausage in a cool place for a few days before smoking.

Smoking Time

Some of the sausages you will smoke, others you won't, and some you will experiment with! Most of the smoking will be cool smoking for a long period of time, as with dry sausage not more than 24 hours at 90°F. or until the sausage turns a rich amber color. When making semidry sausage, you will smoke them for a short amount of time, beginning with a temperature of 120°F. for four hours, then increasing to 150°F. for another four hours. If you are using muslin casing, smoke the sausage until the muslin turns a rich dark brown.

Then you will be ready to air-dry the sausage in a cool, clean place for one to six months. A temperature of 40°F. or below is necessary. This happens to be one of the problems with making your own dried sausage. It's possible to dry it in your own refrigerator if you don't mind the smelling it without tasting it for six months and the inconvenience of the whole thing. A second refrigerator would be even better. Adjust the temperature to 35°–38° with an accurate thermometer. Check the temperature two or three days before you plan on using it. This temperature should remain fairly consistent throughout the drying cycle. Be sure to hang the sausages separately so the air can circulate freely around them.

You will find that within 90 days or so, depending on drying conditions, that the sausages will be pretty dry. This drying process should remove 35% to 45% of the moisture from the meat. The casing will become shriveled and the texture of the sausage very firm, with an aroma that will fill your mouth with moisture!

The type of casing used will determine the exact drying time. Pig casing is not as thick or as heavy as beef casing. Therefore, the beef casing will dry more slowly than the pig casing.

I'm afraid at this point you will have to rely on your own judgment as to whether the sausage is ready, and there is no rule of thumb. But I can tell you that if there is a continual stream of air around the sausage, it tends to dry the outside but not the inside, so no big winds. Dry sausages need no refrigeration. I suggest storing them in a cool place.

The semidry sausage is prepared in much the same manner as the dry sausage, except for the difference in the smoking procedure. They are heated in the smokehouse to fully cook the meat and partially dry it (an internal temperature of 140° is necessary), then they should be allowed to age in a cool place for 30 to 45 days. This type of sausage does need refrigeration after the aging period is complete.

Preserving Dry Sausage

All of the recipes for dry and semidry sausage have salt added. The salt acts as a cure for the meat, a very important part of the preserving process. The other spices make the principal contribution to the final flavor, adding only minutely to the preserving qualities of the finished product.

Here are a few final notes to keep in mind when drying your own sausage.

Salt

Used for its preservative and antiseptic qualities. Also salt draws the moisture from the meat and, because bacteria needs moisture to survive, hinders the growth of bacteria.

Temperature

Keeping the meat below 40°F. inhibits the growth of most bacteria; if maintaining this temperature is impossible and you just have to make some dry sausage, try adding an additional teaspoon of salt per pound of meat and dry in a cool, well-ventilated room, not your attic.

Alcohol

Has antibacterial properties that will certainly stop bacterial growth. It adds flavor and personality to the sausage.

Smoking

Adds flavor; hot smoking as a way of cooking the sausage has only minor preserving qualities.

You may want to experiment in developing your own personal recipes of dry sausage. You can try various combinations of meat, adding different seasonings, trying longer or shorter drying times, changing the grinding procedure and just any number of variations you can conjure up! Be sure to remember to include the cure for the meat, otherwise your sausage may not contain enough salt to stop spoilage. Also, make sure you tightly pack the casing, no air bubbles. Prick them with a pin if you find any.

Included in this book are some recipes that have been around for a long time. Try them and you will find the hardest part is waiting until they have dried long enough to be just right!

Beef Salami

5 lbs. medium ground beef
    chuck
4 Tbsp. salt
1 Tbsp. black pepper
10 cloves pressed garlic

¾ tsp. nutmeg
1 cup red wine
3 tsp. mustard seed
2 Tbsp. sugar

Combine all ingredients, mix well and refrigerate for 48 hours. Stuff into beef or fiber casing. Tie off into 10-inch links. Dry for 10–12 weeks.

AMERICAN

Missouri Dried Sausage

4 lbs. medium ground beef
    chuck
1 lb. fine ground pork butt
4 Tbsp. salt

4 Tbsp. sugar
1 Tbsp. black pepper
1 cup brandy

Combine all ingredients, mix well and refrigerate for 48 hours. Stuff into fiber or beef casing. Dry approximately 5–9 weeks. Smoke this sausage with a heavy cool smoke (approximately 48 hours).

AMERICAN

Chinese Sausage

5 lbs. coarse ground pork butt	⅓ cup sugar
4 Tbsp. salt	1 cup soy sauce
	1 cup rice wine

Combine all ingredients, mix well and refrigerate for 48 hours. Stuff into hog casing, tie in 5- to 6-inch links. Dry for 6–10 weeks. Can be cool smoked (24 hours, lightly).

CHINESE

Chinese Szechuan Sausage

5 lbs. coarse ground pork butt	2 Tbsp. crushed red pepper (hot)
3 Tbsp. salt	1 tsp. ginger
1 cup soy sauce	1 cup rice wine
2 Tbsp. sugar	
10 cloves pressed garlic	

Combine all ingredients, mix well and refrigerate for 48 hours. Stuff into hog casing and tie in 4-inch links. Dry for 6–10 weeks.

CHINESE

Dry Cervelat

2 lbs. medium ground beef
  chuck
2 lbs. medium ground pork
  butt
1 lb. medium ground bacon
1 small grated onion

6 cloves pressed garlic
1½ Tbsp. coarsely ground
  black pepper
3 Tbsp. salt
1 cup dry white wine

Combine all ingredients and mix well. Allow to cure 48 hours
in the refrigerator. Stuff into casing. Tie approximately 4 or 5
inches in length. Dry from 3–4 weeks. Boil a mixture of white
wine, thyme, sage and bay leaf. Rub the sausage with this and
allow to dry another 4 weeks.

FRENCH

Lyon Sausage

 5 lbs. medium ground pork
   butt
10 cloves pressed garlic

1½ Tbsp. white pepper
 4 Tbsp. salt
 1 cup white wine

Combine all ingredients, mix well and refrigerate for 48 hours.
Stuff into hog casing and tie in 8-inch links. Hang in a cool place
for 12–16 weeks.

4 lbs. medium ground pork
   butt
1 lb. medium ground bacon
2 Tbsp. sugar
4 Tbsp. salt

1½ tsp. white pepper
1 tsp. white peppercorns
1 tsp. quatre-épices
1 cup white wine

Combine all ingredients, mix well and refrigerate for 48 hours. Stuff into beef casing and tie in 18-inch links. Hang in a cool place for 12–16 weeks.

FRENCH

Saucisson D'Aries

3 lbs. fine ground pork butt
1 lb. medium ground bacon
1 lb. medium ground beef
   chuck
4 Tbsp. salt

2 Tbsp. sugar
2 tsp. black pepper
2 tsp. whole black pepper
2 tsp. quatre-épices
1 cup vodka

Combine all ingredients, mix well and refrigerate for 48 hours. Stuff into beef casing, tie every 18 inches. Dry for approximately 16–20 weeks.

FRENCH

Saucisson De Campagne

5 lbs. medium ground pork
   butt
4 Tbsp. salt
1 tsp. sugar

1 tsp. black pepper
1 tsp. quatre-épices
1 cup red wine

Combine all ingredients, mix well and refrigerate for 48 hours. Stuff into large hog or beef casing. Tie off every 6–8 inches and dry for 6–8 weeks.

FRENCH

Saucisson Au Foie De Pork

2 lbs. fine ground pork butt
2 lbs. cooked pork liver,
   mashed
1 lb. cooked beef tongue, cubed
4 Tbsp. salt
1 cup chopped onions

1 Tbsp. black pepper
3 tsp. quatre-épices
2 cups chopped mushrooms or
   truffles
4 oz. pistachio nuts, blanched
1 cup white wine or brandy

Combine all ingredients, mix well and refrigerate for 48 hours. Stuff into hog casing, tie off every 4–6 inches. Simmer for 1 hour. Dry 6–10 weeks.

FRENCH

Saucisson À L'Ail

5 lbs. medium ground pork
    butt
4 Tbsp. salt
1 tsp. black pepper
1 tsp. whole black pepper

1 tsp. quatre-épices
1 tsp. cayenne pepper
8 cloves pressed garlic
1 cup brandy

Combine all ingredients, mix well and refrigerate for 48 hours. Stuff into beef casing. Tie every 10–12 inches. Dry for 20 weeks.

FRENCH

Saucisson De Lorraine

3 lbs. fine ground pork butt
2 lbs. medium ground beef
    chuck
4 Tbsp. salt

3 tsp. sugar
2 tsp. black pepper
2 tsp. quatre-épices
1 cup brandy

Combine all ingredients, mix well and refrigerate for 48 hours. Stuff into beef casing, tie every 18 inches. Dry for approximately 16–20 weeks.

FRENCH

Saucisson De Ménage

5 lbs. medium ground pork
    butt
4 Tbsp. salt
2 tsp. black pepper

2 tsp. quatre-épices
10 cloves pressed garlic
1 cup red wine

Combine all ingredients, mix well and refrigerate for 48 hours. Stuff into large hog casing, tie every 8 inches. Dry for approximately 8–12 weeks.

FRENCH

Saucisson De Ménage Fumé

5 lbs. medium ground pork
    butt
4 Tbsp. salt
2 Tbsp. sugar

1½ Tbsp. black pepper
1 Tbsp. quatre-épices
5 cloves pressed garlic
1 cup brandy

Combine all ingredients, mix well and refrigerate for 48 hours. Stuff into beef casing. Cool smoke for 48 hours or until it is a deep yellow-brown. Dry 6–8 weeks.

FRENCH

Saucisson Á Trancher

5 lbs. *fine ground pork butt*
4 Tbsp. *salt*
3 tsp. *black pepper*
3 tsp. *quatre-épices*

6 *cloves pressed garlic*
½ *cup chopped parsley*
1 *cup white wine*

Combine all ingredients, mix well and refrigerate for 48 hours. Stuff into large hog casing. Dry 6–8 weeks.

FRENCH

Angburgerwurst

4 lbs. *coarse ground pork butt*
1 lb. *coarse ground bacon*
4 Tbsp. *salt*
3 Tbsp. *sugar*

1 Tbsp. *black pepper*
1 tsp. *ground cloves*
2 tsp. *ground nutmeg*
1 *cup water*

Combine all ingredients, mix well and refrigerate for 48 hours. Stuff into hog casing, and cool smoke with a heavy smoke for 3 hours. Dry for approximately 6–8 weeks.

GERMAN

Landjaeger

3 lbs. *medium ground beef*
    chuck
2 lbs. *medium ground pork*
    butt
1½ Tbsp. *white pepper*

1 tsp. *caraway seed*
8 *cloves pressed garlic*
2 Tbsp. *sugar*
4 Tbsp. *salt*
1 cup *Rhine wine*

Combine all ingredients and mix well. Allow to cure 48 hours in the refrigerator. Stuff loosely into hog casing. Tie links every 6 inches. Flatten the sausages by squeezing between two boards. Leave them until they have set their shape permanently (approximately 24 hours). Cool smoke 24 hours and air dry thoroughly (approximately 10–12 weeks).

GERMAN

German Salami

2½ lbs. *coarse ground beef*
    chuck
2½ lbs. *medium ground pork*
    butt
4 Tbsp. *salt*

2 Tbsp. *sugar*
8 *cloves pressed garlic*
1 Tbsp. *white pepper*
1 cup *Rhine wine*

Combine all ingredients, mix well and refrigerate for 48 hours. Stuff into large hog or beef casing. Dry for 9–12 weeks. This sausage can be smoked if you like (about 24 hours). Cold smoke before drying.

GERMAN

Summer Sausage

3 lbs. medium ground beef
chuck
2 lbs. fine ground pork butt
4 Tbsp. salt
1½ Tbsp. black pepper

3 tsp. sage
1 Tbsp. sugar
8 cloves pressed garlic
1 cup Rhine wine

Combine all ingredients, mix well and refrigerate for 48 hours. Stuff into hog casing and tie off every 5 inches. Dry for 8–12 weeks.

GERMAN

Thuringer

Combine all ingredients, mix well and refrigerate for 48 hours. Stuff into large hog casing, and cool smoke with a heavy smoke for 6–8 hours. Dry for approximately 6–8 weeks.

5 lbs. fine ground pork butt
4 Tbsp. salt
1 Tbsp. black pepper

½ tsp. ground ginger
3 Tbsp. sugar
1 cup Rhine wine

3 lbs. fine ground beef chuck
2 lbs. fine ground pork butt
4 Tbsp. salt
1 Tbsp. white pepper
1 Tbsp. sugar

1 Tbsp. paprika
1 tsp. celery seed
1 tsp. coriander
1 tsp. crushed caraway seed
1 cup Rhine wine

GERMAN

Kosher Salami

Combine all ingredients, mix well and refrigerate for 48 hours. Stuff into fiber or cellulose casing. Cool smoke for 6–8 hours. Slowly increase the temperature to 150°–160°F. or until the internal temperature is 140°F. Chill the sausage in cold water and continue to dry (approximately 5–8 weeks).

5 lbs. medium ground beef
    chuck
4 Tbsp. salt
3 Tbsp. sugar
1 Tbsp. black pepper

1 Tbsp. paprika
2 tsp. ground ginger
1 tsp. nutmeg
8 cloves pressed garlic
1 cup white wine

5 lbs. medium ground beef
   chuck
1 Tbsp. white pepper
1 tsp. ground coriander
½ tsp. nutmeg

½ tsp. cardamom
8 cloves pressed garlic
1 Tbsp. sugar
4 Tbsp. salt
1 cup white wine

5 lbs. fine ground beef chuck
4 Tbsp. salt
10 cloves pressed garlic
1½ tsp. white pepper

3 tsp. ground coriander
1 Tbsp. sugar
1 cup white wine

ISRAELI

Calabrese Salami

5 lbs. medium ground pork
   butt
4 Tbsp. salt
2 tsp. fennel
1 Tbsp. white pepper

3 Tbsp. crushed red peppers
   (hot)
½ cup sweet vermouth
½ cup brandy
6 cloves pressed garlic

Combine all ingredients, mix well and refrigerate for 48 hours.

Stuff into large hog casing and tie off into 8-inch links. Dry for
10–12 weeks.

ITALIAN

Capicola

5 lbs. diced pork butt (¾ to 1 inch cubes)	4 Tbsp. paprika
	2 Tbsp. ground red pepper
4 Tbsp. salt	1 cup red wine
1 Tbsp. sugar	

Combine all ingredients, mix well and refrigerate for 48 hours.
Stuff into beef casing and dry approximately 12–16 weeks. Can
be lightly smoked.

ITALIAN

Catania Salami

5 lbs. medium ground pork butt	½ Tbsp. white pepper
	¼ tsp. nutmeg
4 Tbsp. salt	½ tsp. ground coriander
2 Tbsp. sugar	1 tsp. fennel
1 Tbsp. black pepper	1 cup sweet vermouth

Combine all ingredients, mix well and refrigerate for 48 hours.
Stuff into beef or fiber casing, and tie off into 10-inch links. Dry
for 10–12 weeks.

ITALIAN

Genoa Salami

2½ lbs. *fine ground beef chuck*
2½ lbs. *fine ground pork butt*
4 Tbsp. *salt*
1½ Tbsp. *sugar*
1 Tbsp. *black peppercorns*
1 Tbsp. *white pepper*

½ tsp. *ground coriander*
10 *cloves pressed garlic*
½ tsp. *cardamom*
½ cup *red wine*
½ cup *brandy*

Combine all ingredients, mix well and refrigerate for 48 hours. Stuff into beef or fiber casing. Tie off in 12-inch links. Dry for 10–14 weeks.

5 lbs. *medium ground beef chuck*
4 Tbsp. *salt*
1 Tbsp. *sugar*

1 Tbsp. *whole black pepper*
3 tsp. *white pepper*
10 *cloves pressed garlic*
1 cup *red wine*

Combine all ingredients, mix well and refrigerate for 48 hours. Stuff into beef or fiber casing. Dry for approximately 10–14 weeks.

ITALIAN

Hard Salami

2 lbs. *fine ground beef chuck*
3 lbs. *fine ground pork butt*
5 Tbsp. *salt*
4 Tbsp. *sugar*

1 Tbsp. *white pepper*
½ tsp. *ginger*
10 *cloves pressed garlic*
1 cup *red wine*

Combine all ingredients, mix well and refrigerate for 48 hours. Stuff into fiber casing or beef casing. Dry approximately 12–15 weeks.

ITALIAN

Italian Dry Sausage

5 lbs. medium ground pork butt	1 tsp. anise
4 Tbsp. salt	10 cloves pressed garlic
1 Tbsp. sugar	1 Tbsp. crushed red pepper (hot)
3 tsp. fennel	1 cup red wine

Combine all ingredients, mix well and refrigerate for 48 hours. Stuff into hog casing. Tie off into 4- to 5-inch links. Dry for 8–10 weeks.

ITALIAN

Italian Mild Salami

2½ lbs. medium ground beef chuck	1 tsp. cayenne pepper
2½ lbs. medium ground pork butt	1 tsp. ground fennel
4 Tbsp. salt	1 Tbsp. sugar
1 Tbsp. black pepper	8 cloves pressed garlic
1 Tbsp. white pepper	1 tsp. coriander
	1 cup red wine
	½ cup brandy

Combine all ingredients, mix well and refrigerate for 48 hours. Stuff into large hog casing. Tie off every 8—10 inches. Dry for 12 weeks.

ITALIAN

Italian Salami

1 lb. *medium ground beef chuck*	3 tsp. *crushed red pepper*
4 lbs. *fine ground pork butt*	2 Tbsp. *sugar*
1½ Tbsp. *white pepper*	10 cloves *pressed garlic*
4 Tbsp. *salt*	1 cup *red wine*

Combine all ingredients, mix well and refrigerate for 48 hours. Stuff into large hog casing. Dry for 9–12 weeks.

ITALIAN

Milano Salami

2 lbs. *medium ground beef chuck*	2 Tbsp. *sugar*
3 lbs. *medium ground pork butt*	1 Tbsp. *white pepper*
	1 Tbsp. *whole white pepper*
4 Tbsp. *salt*	8 cloves *pressed garlic*
	1 cup *red wine*

Combine all ingredients, mix well and allow to cure 48 hours in the refrigerator before stuffing into large hog or beef casing. Dry for 9–10 weeks.

ITALIAN

Mortadella

Combine all ingredients, mix well and refrigerate for 48 hours. Traditionally, Mortadella is stuffed into a pig's bladder, which is hard to find, so I'll use beef casing. Cold smoke for 72 hours. Dry from 6–10 weeks.

3 lbs. medium ground pork butt
2 lbs. cubed bacon (½ inch cubes)
4 Tbsp. salt
3 tsp. peppercorns

2 tsp. white pepper
2 tsp. coriander
½ tsp. cloves
½ tsp. cinnamon
1 cup white wine

3 lbs. medium ground pork butt
2 lbs. medium ground veal
4 Tbsp. salt
2 Tbsp. ginger

2 Tbsp. nutmeg
2 Tbsp. cinnamon
1 Tbsp. black pepper
2 cups red wine

ITALIAN

Pepperoni

Combine all ingredients, mix well and refrigerate for 48 hours. Stuff into hog casing. Tie off into 10-inch links. Dry for 6–10 weeks.

2 lbs. coarse ground beef chuck
3 lbs. medium ground pork
   butt
4 Tbsp. salt
1 Tbsp. sugar

1 Tbsp. cayenne
2 Tbsp. paprika
2 tsp. crushed anise seed
8 cloves pressed garlic
1 cup red wine

2½ lbs. medium ground beef
   chuck
2½ lbs. fine ground pork butt
5 Tbsp. salt
1 Tbsp. sugar
3 tsp. black pepper

1 Tbsp. crushed red peppers
   (hot)
½ tsp. allspice
2½ tsp. crushed anise seed
1 cup red wine

5 lbs. medium ground beef
   chuck
4 Tbsp. salt
1½ Tbsp. black pepper
3 tsp. mustard seed
3 tsp. fennel seed, crushed

2 tsp. crushed red pepper
   (hot)
1½ tsp. anise seed
6 cloves pressed garlic
1 cup red wine

ITALIAN

Soppresatta Salami

2 lbs. coarse ground beef chuck
3 lbs. medium ground pork
  butt
4 Tbsp. salt
1 Tbsp. black pepper

2 tsp. white pepper
½ tsp. ground coriander
2 tsp. sugar
10 cloves pressed garlic
1 cup red wine

Combine all ingredients, mix well and refrigerate for 48 hours.
Stuff into large hot or beef casing. Dry for 8–12 weeks.

ITALIAN

Dry Chorizo

5 lbs. coarse ground pork butt
4 Tbsp. salt
1 Tbsp. black pepper
2 Tbsp. cayenne
1 Tbsp. crushed red pepper
  (hot)
14 cloves pressed garlic

1 tsp. fennel
1 tsp. oregano
1 tsp. cumin
4 Tbsp. paprika
½ cup wine vinegar
½ cup brandy

Combine all ingredients, mix well and refrigerate for 48 hours.
Stuff into large hog casing. Tie off into 4-inch links. Dry for
8–10 weeks.

SPANISH

Göteborg Sausage

Combine all ingredients, mix well and refrigerate for 48 hours. Stuff into beef or fiber casing. Cool smoke with a heavy smoke for 8–12 hours. Dry for 10–12 weeks.

3 lbs. medium ground beef chuck
2 lbs. fine ground pork butt
4 Tbsp. salt
1 Tbsp. black pepper

2 Tbsp. ground mustard
1 Tbsp. nutmeg
6 cloves pressed garlic
2 Tbsp. sugar
1 cup dry sherry

3 lbs. medium ground beef chuck
2 lbs. fine ground pork butt
4 Tbsp. salt

1 Tbsp. black pepper
1 Tbsp. thyme
2 tsp. cardamom
1 cup dry sherry

SWEDISH

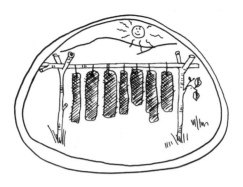

11

Jerky Recipes

I FEEL THAT a cookbook on sausage making would not be complete if it didn't include the various ways of making jerky. This is a preserving process and the result is *so* tasty! Jerky is also a little easier to make than sausage and needs no refrigeration. This delicious food has a high nutritional value, lacking only in Vitamin C and animal fat. It can be made from almost any kind of meat you have available. I would suggest staying away from pork and fowl.

Did you know that jerky is simply dried, uncooked meat? That's right, just raw meat! It takes about four pounds of raw meat to make one pound of jerky, which makes it one of the most concentrated edibles known to man. This delicacy can be eaten alone or cut into paper-thin slices and creamed as you would make creamed chopped beef or even a delectable stew. It's great any way you eat it!

Methods of Preparation

Now, the secret of making your very own jerky is in the way you cut the meat. Work with almost-frozen meat and cut it lengthwise with the grain for a chewy texture or across the grain for more tenderness. Use only muscle meat, trimming off all visible fat before drying! Fat left in the meat will turn rancid. Flank meat is great for use in making jerky. Cut the meat into strips approximately 3⁄16" to 1⁄4" thick and about 1½" to 2" wide, cutting the strips as long as possible. Season with salt and pepper. If you prefer more flavor, use a little oregano, marjoram, basil, thyme, or whatever other spice might tempt your palate. Use more seasoning than you think necessary, as the drying process will weaken the flavor of the spices. You will have to rub or pound the seasonings into the meat. If using a wooden mallet to pound in the seasonings, be careful not to break the meat apart in the process.

Another way of preparing jerky is to soak the meat strips in a brine consisting of one pound of salt, 4 ounces of sugar, two crushed cloves of garlic dissolved in one gallon of water. Soak in the brine for about 12 to 14 hours, then wash in cold water, and dry with a towel. Season to your taste and smoke until dry, or dry without smoke. Or you can try marinating jerky. Put the meat strips in a plastic bag, pour in the marinade, squeeze out all air, and seal the bag. Refrigerate and periodically change the position of the bag. Soak in the marinade for approximately 12 hours, then remove the strips from the bag and proceed with the drying.

Rack Drying

The drying rack can be built from almost anything as long as the following conditions are met.

1) The strips of meat must not touch one another.
2) You must cover the rack with a clean light cloth or wire screen which will act as a deterrent to dirt and flies.

3) The meat must be protected from the moist night air and from rain.

I have found a moveable rack to be the most convenient. Whatever works best for you is what you should use.

Attach a string to one end of each strip of meat and hang from a rack in the sun to dry. Remember to keep the meat separated on the drying racks. To test the jerky for doneness, if you are drying it in the sun, bend a slice. The jerky should crack when bent but not break—jerky should not be brittle. Keep in mind the jerky will turn more brittle as it cools off. Please note: when sun drying jerky, spoilage and contamination are very high.

Smoke Drying

You may be a little more of a pioneer than most people and want to build a smokey fire under the drying meat. Use non-resinous woods when making your fire. Apple, hickory, or cherry woods are ideal. The smoke definitely adds more flavor to the meat, but does entail a little more time than the rack drying method.

Smoking jerky must be done in the early part of the drying process, and the smoke must be around 120°–140°F. Smoke the meat at this temperature until the jerky will pass the test for dryness. The smoke will keep most bugs away and also inhibits the growth of some surface bacteria.

Oven Drying

If you really don't want to go to all the trouble of watching and caring for the meat while it is in the sun or drying above a fire or in a smokehouse, you can try the old oven method. It's really very simple to do.

Cut the meat along the grain into strips about 3/16″ to 1/4″ thick and 1 1/2″ wide and season to your taste. You can add liquid smoke or smoke-flavor salt to oven-dried jerky. Lay the strips out on oven racks, put foil under the racks to catch the drippings, and turn the heat to approximately 140°F. Let the oven door remain partially open to let the moisture out. Four hours later you turn the whole works over. The meat is *not* supposed to cook, just dry out. Don't hurry the procedure. Making jerky is a *drying* and not a cooking process. Give it another four hours and take a look. If the meat has shriveled up, turned blackish-red, and looks like shoe leather, you can figure it's just about right. It should take approximately 10 to 15 hours. If there is no moisture in the center of the pieces and the jerky is flexible enough to bend without snapping, then it's ready to make its way to your drooling mouth!

Making Pemmican

I'd like to share with you the method of preparing pemmican. It's a fantastic trail food, though it's good any other time too. Pemmican was originated by the North American Indians and contains every necessary mineral, vitamin, and food element, with the exception of Vitamin C, and is prepared with, you guessed it, jerky! It will keep for months without refrigeration and indefinitely in a cool, dry place.

To prepare pemmican, pound and shred apart as much jerky as you desire. Add raisins, dried or chopped berries, dried fruit. Mix thoroughly and there it is.

Pemmican may be eaten as is, or you can add water and/or heat if you prefer. The American Indians added melted animal fat and patted the mixture into cakes for trail use. I do not suggest this—however, for whatever use you can make of it, here is a two-hundred-year-old recipe right at your fingertips!

Storage

Store the jerky in a glass mason jar with a perforated lid or any other glass jar with a lid that you have available. It will keep 2 to 3 months if kept in a cool place or in a refrigerator and it can be frozen.

Jerky Marinades

(Marinade recipes for approx. 5 lbs. of beef or venison: marinate for approx. 12–24 hours)

Spanish Style

5 tsp. salt
1½ tsp. black pepper
2 Tbsp. coriander
1½ tsp. chili powder

1½ tsp. ground ginger
1½ tsp. turmeric
1½ tsp. ground cumin

New York Style

5 tsp. salt
⅓ cup Worcestershire sauce

1 finely chopped onion
2 tsp. black pepper

Brownsville Style

5 tsp. salt
2 tsp. black pepper
5 tsp. chili powder
4 cloves pressed garlic

1½ tsp. crushed hot peppers
3 tsp. crushed oregano
5 tsp. paprika

Easy Style

5 tsp. salt
2 tsp. black pepper
¼ cup brown sugar

1½ cup soy sauce
1 cup red wine vinegar

Lincoln Style

5 tsp. salt
5 tsp. basil
5 cloves pressed garlic

1½ tsp. crushed oregano
1½ tsp. parsley, chopped

Boston Style

1 cup soy sauce
⅓ cup Worcestershire sauce
1½ tsp. black pepper
1 finely chopped onion

5 cloves pressed garlic
1 tsp. ground nutmeg
1 tsp. ground ginger

Creole Style

5 tsp. salt
1½ tsp. black pepper
1½ tsp. cayenne pepper
1 minced onion

3 tsp. paprika
10 cloves pressed garlic
1 cup red wine vinegar
1 cup Worcestershire sauce

Mexican Style

5 tsp. salt
1½ tsp. black pepper
⅓ cup chili powder

8 cloves pressed garlic
1 minced onion
1½ tsp. ground cumin

Ohio Style

5 tsp. salt
1½ tsp. black pepper
5 cloves pressed garlic

½ cup Worcestershire sauce
½ cup liquid smoke

Tex-Mex Style

5 tsp. salt
1½ tsp. black pepper
1½ tsp. cayenne pepper
1 finely chopped onion
5 cloves pressed garlic

5 tsp. dry mustard
1 cup brown sugar
1½ cups red wine vinegar
1 cup catsup

China Sauce

5 tsp. salt
1½ tsp. black pepper
1 large minced onion
5 cloves pressed garlic

1 cup brown sugar
⅓ cup soy sauce
1¼ cups red wine
1½ cups pineapple juice

Delhi Style

5 tsp. salt
1½ tsp. black pepper
½ tsp. cinnamon
¼ tsp. ground cloves
½ tsp. cumin

3 tsp. curry powder
4 cloves pressed garlic
3 tsp. ground ginger
1 cup cream sherry

New Mexico Style

3½ tsp. salt
1½ tsp. black pepper
⅓ cup brown sugar

5 cloves pressed garlic
¾ cup soy sauce
⅓ cup Worcestershire sauce

Guadalajara Style

1½ cups "your pick" barbecue
   sauce
3 Tbsp. liquid smoke

2 tsp. chili powder
1½ Tbsp. Worcestershire sauce
1 tsp. cayenne pepper

Italian Style

1 cup Worcestershire sauce
1½ cups soy sauce
3 Tbsp. tomato sauce
3 Tbsp. red wine vinegar

3 tsp. sugar
5 cloves pressed garlic
1 small chopped onion
1 tsp. salt

Early American Style

6 tsp. black pepper   2 cups beef bouillon (4 cubes)
6 tsp. salt

Southern California Style

1½ cups soy sauce   1 tsp. nutmeg
  5 Tbsp. Worcestershire sauce   1 tsp. ginger
1½ tsp. black pepper   10 tsp. liquid smoke
  4 cloves pressed garlic   5 tsp. crushed peppers, dried
  ¼ tsp. powdered onions

Hawaiian Style—Oahu

2½ tsp. salt   ¾ Tbsp. brown sugar
  1 tsp. black pepper   5 cloves pressed garlic
2½ tsp. ground ginger   1½ cups soy sauce

Hawaiian Style—Kaula

  2 cups soy sauce   3 tsp. ginger
⅓ cup salt   4 cloves pressed garlic
  1 Tbsp. sugar   2 tsp. black pepper

Hawaiian Style—Maui

5 tsp. salt	1 tsp. cayenne pepper
5 tsp. ground ginger	6 cloves pressed garlic
5 Tbsp. brown sugar	1½ cups pineapple juice
1½ tsp. black pepper	1½ cups soy sauce

Sausage Suppliers

Grinders

Cook's Mart
609 N. LaSalle Street
Chicago, Illinois 60610

H. Roth and Son
177 First Avenue
New York, New York 10028

Rowoco
111 Calvert Street
Harrison, New York 10528

Casings

Richard S. Kutas
1067 Grant Street
Buffalo, New York 14207

Rothamer Meats
Rt. 1
Cottage Grove, Wisconsin
53527

Sedro Industries
P.O. Box 8009
Rochester, New York 14606

Standard Casing Company
121 Spring Street
New York, New York 10012

Spices

Cuisine Market Place
133 B.W. DeLaGuerra Street
Santa Barbara, California
93101

Richard Kutas
1067 Grant Street
Buffalo, New York 14207

Morton Salt Company
Chicago, Illinois 60606

Paprikas Weiss
1546 Second Avenue
New York, New York 10028

Additional Resources

American Association for World Health, 2121 Virginia Ave. N.W., Washington, D.C. 20037.

American Meat Institute, P.O. Box 3556, Washington, D.C. 20007.

Gehman, Richard, *The Signet Book of Sausage*, New York: The New American Library, 1976.

George A. Hormel & Co., 501 16th Ave. N.E., Austin, Minnesota 55912.

Gourmet, Gourmet Inc., 777 Third Ave., New York, New York 10017.

Morton Salt Division, Morton-Norwich Products, Inc., 110 N. Wacker Dr., Chicago, Illinois 60606.

National Live Stock & Meat Board, 444 N. Michigan Ave., Chicago, Illinois 60611.

North Carolina Agricultural & Technical State University, 312 N. Dudley St., Greensboro, North Carolina 27411.

Oregon State University, Cooperative Ext. Service, Corvallis, Oregon 97331.

Sleight, Jack and Hull, Raymond, *The Homebook of Smoke Cooking, Meat, Fish, and Game*, Harrisburg, Pa: Stackpole Books, 1971.

Swift & Company, 115 W. Jackson Blvd., Chicago, Illinois 60604.

United States Department of Agriculture, Washington, D.C. 20251.

University of California Agricultural Ext., Berkeley, California 94720, C/O College of Agricultural Sciences.

Index

179